US Quidditch
RULEBOOK

Tenth Edition

Image credits

Cover image © Isabella Gong
Images on pp. 10, 42, 132, & 222 © Jessica Jiamin Lang
Images on pg. 14, 74, & 218 © Sofia de la Vega
Image on pg. 20 © Nicole Harrig
Images on pp. 84 & 176 © Matt Dwyer
Image on pg. 204 © Monica Wheeler
Cover design by Alicia Radford
Diagrams by Mary Kimball, Crystal Hutcheson, and Katie Bone
Referee signals by Eric Andres

Published by US Quidditch, Inc.

ISBN-10: 1534832459
ISBN-13: 978-1534832459

To learn more about USQ, visit www.usquidditch.org

This rulebook is the result of the hard work of many people. We would like to thank everyone who has given input and insight to make it the best it can be. Particular thanks to the following people for their work creating and editing the rulebook:

Michael Clark-Polner

Kym Couch

Clay Dockery

Dan Hanson

Nicole Harrig

Cindy Holden

Mary Kimball

Sarah Kneiling

Jared Leggett

Caleb Ragatz

Devin Sandon

Eric Schnier

Sarah Woolsey

Thanks also to the authors of previous editions, including Xander Manshel, Alex Benepe, Jared Kowalczyk, and Will Hack.

Contents

Contents continued

About US Quidditch

Our mission

US Quidditch (USQ) is the national governing body for the sport of quidditch. USQ advances the sport by organizing events and programs that build community and empower all genders to compete together.

Our vision

We envision a future where every person in the United States is aware of quidditch as a sport and has opportunities to play and engage at all levels.

Our core values

- We establish the foundation for long-term sustainability through regulations, innovation, and expansion.
- We provide competitive opportunities for every level of athlete.
- We build a safe, inclusive, and respectful community.
- We strive to be a leader in gender inclusivity for all age groups.
- We create meaningful community partnerships.
- We develop and empower future leaders.

A 501(c)3 nonprofit founded in 2010, US Quidditch serves over 4,000 athletes on almost 200 teams nationwide and provides a range of services, from hosting nine major tournaments and supervising regular season competition, to training and certifying referees, snitches, and tournament directors, offering grants, and working to expand the sport into younger age groups through outreach programs at the elementary, middle, and high school levels. Learn more at www.usquidditch.org.

The gender maximum rule

A quidditch game allows each team to have a maximum of four players who identify as the same gender in active play on the field at the same time. This number increases to five once the seekers enter the game. The gender that a player identifies with is considered to be that player's gender, which may or may not correspond with that person's sex. This is commonly referred to as the gender maximum rule.

USQ accepts those who don't identify within the binary gender system and acknowledges that not all of our players identify as male or female. USQ welcomes people of all identities and genders into our league.

Introduction

The sport of quidditch continues to grow in popularity and mature as a dynamic and competitive game involving intense physicality, complex strategy, and immense skill.

As the sport expands and evolves, it is the responsibility of the rulebook to keep up by addressing challenges, issues, and new methods of play. The rulebook must be proactive and able to address the safety and gameplay concerns of a sport that continues to evolve at a rapid and unpredictable pace.

Quidditch is no longer merely a backyard sport: it can be played in an open field or before an audience of thousands. Whatever the conditions of play, the rulebook needs to have a consistent answer for how the game must work.

The tenth edition of the USQ rulebook attempts to address those areas in which the rulebook displayed inconsistency and needed additional clarification. We hope that this edition continues to provide greater clarity and consistency than ever before. The rules will never be perfect, but the goal of this rulebook is to provide the most consistent and easily replicable set of rules and regulations yet.

For those of you who are new to the sport of quidditch, we recommend that you learn the basic rules from your friends, teammates, and the overview in 1.1. Quidditch: An overview before you read straight through this rulebook. Of course, the more ambitious among you are welcome to dive right in!

1. Basics of the Game

1.1. QUIDDITCH: AN OVERVIEW

Quidditch is a gender-integrated contact sport with a unique mix of elements from rugby, dodgeball, wrestling, flag football, and other sports. A quidditch team is made up of at least seven athletes who play with brooms between their legs at all times. While the game can appear chaotic to the casual observer, once familiar with the basic rules, quidditch is an exciting sport to watch and even more exciting to play.

1.2. POSITIONS OVERVIEW

Each team has three chasers, two beaters, and one keeper in play at all times. Each team sends one seeker into the game at the end of the seeker floor (See: 3.4.1.2. Seeker floor).

1.2.1. Chaser overview

Chasers in play per team: Three
Game ball used: Quaffle
Headband color: White
Objective: Throw, kick, or in any way pass the quaffle through the opposing team's hoops to score ten points.

1.2.2. Keeper overview

Keepers in play per team: One

Game ball used: Quaffle

Headband color: Green

Objective: Prevent opponents from throwing, kicking or otherwise propelling the quaffle through their team's hoops.

1.2.3. Beater overview

Beaters in play per team: Two

Game ball used: Bludger

Headband color: Black

Objective: Throw, kick, or in any way propel the bludgers to disrupt the flow of the game by "knocking out" other players.

1.2.4. Seeker overview

Seekers in play per team: One

Game ball used: Snitch

Headband color: Yellow

Objective: Remove the snitch ball from the snitch runner to score 30 points and end the period.

1.3. GAMEPLAY OVERVIEW

1.3.1. Quaffle players

A. The chasers and keepers, also known as quaffle players, attempt to score goals, and prevent the other team from scoring goals, with the quaffle. Goals are worth ten points each.

B. Quaffle players advance the ball down the field by running with it, passing it to teammates, or kicking it.

C. Quaffle players defend by positioning or by initiating various forms of legal physical contact with other quaffle players.

D. While in their team's own keeper zone, the keeper is immune to the knockout effect and has several other specialized powers (See: 7.3.3.2. Keeper-specific powers). During this time, the keeper is considered to be a protected keeper. Otherwise, the keeper position is the same as the chaser position.

1.3.2. Bludger players

A. The beaters use balls called bludgers to disrupt the flow of the game by "knocking out" any player from the opposing team who does not have knockout immunity (See: 5.2.8. Knockout immunity).

B. Any player hit by a bludger propelled by an opponent is out of play until they complete the knockout procedure, unless they have knockout immunity (See: 5.3. Knockout procedure).

1.3.3. Snitch players

A. The seekers try to remove the snitch ball from the snitch runner to score 30 points and end the period.

B. The snitch is a ball attached to the waistband of the snitch runner, a neutral athlete and official dressed in yellow, whose job it is to remain fair to both teams while avoiding capture for as long as possible.

C. Catching the snitch is worth 30 points and its capture ends the period. The three periods are "regulation time," "overtime," and "second overtime." If the score is tied after any snitch catch, the game proceeds into the next period.

1.4. FOULS OVERVIEW

From the time that players enter the player area for a game until after the game has ended, players are forbidden from taking certain actions called fouls. Players who commit a foul face different consequences depending on the severity of the offense.

1.4.1. Back to hoops

A back to hoops foul indicates that a player must cease active play and complete the knockout procedure (See: 5.3. Knockout procedure).

1.4.2. Blue card

A blue card indicates that a player must spend one minute of game time in the penalty box and the player's team must play a player down for this minute. If the opposing team scores before the minute expires, the player may be released early and reenter play. Blue cards do not "stack" to become higher penalties.

1.4.3. Yellow card

A yellow card indicates that a player must spend one minute of game time in the penalty box and the player's team must play a player down for this minute. If the opposing team scores before the minute expires, the player may be released early and reenter play. A player who receives two yellow cards in a single game must be issued a red card.

1.4.4. Red card

A red card indicates that a player is barred from the rest of the game and the player's team must play a player down for two full minutes of game time.

1.4.5. Ejection

A referee may eject a player for egregious violations of the rules.

1.5. THE GENDER MAXIMUM RULE

A quidditch game allows each team to have a maximum of four players who identify as the same gender in active play on the field at the same time. This number increases to five once the seekers enter the game. The gender that a player identifies with is considered to be that player's gender, which may or may not correspond with that person's sex. This is commonly referred to as the gender maximum rule.

USQ accepts those who don't identify within the binary gender system and acknowledges that not all of our players identify as male or female. USQ welcomes people of all identities and genders into our league.

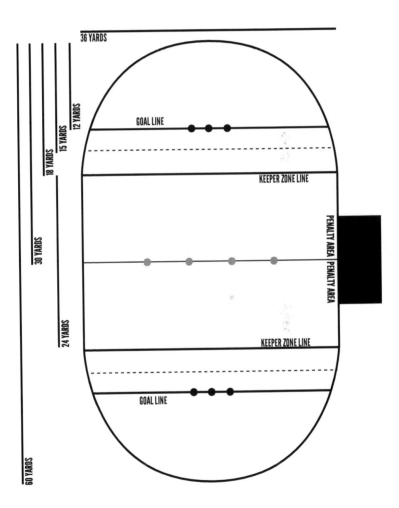

36 YARDS

12 YARDS

15 YARDS

18 YARDS

30 YARDS

24 YARDS

60 YARDS

GOAL LINE

KEEPER ZONE LINE

PENALTY AREA | PENALTY AREA

KEEPER ZONE LINE

GOAL LINE

2.1. THE PITCH

2.1.1. Pitch shape

The pitch is composed of three parts: a rectangle and two semicircles capping the the width of the rectangle. With the semicircles capping the rectangle, the entire pitch is pill-shaped. While these boundaries create the desired shape of the pitch, they do not strictly bind the players to this area.

A. Sidelines and keeper zone lines:
   i. The rectangle forms the main body of the pitch. The vertical straight edges of the rectangle are the sidelines. The horizontal edges of the rectangle are the keeper zone lines.
B. Backlines and backpoints:
   i. A backline is a semicircle which extends from the keeper zone line and joins each end of the same keeper zone line. The midpoint of each backline, the point along this semicircle that is farthest from the keeper zone line, is the backpoint. There are two backlines and two backpoints on a pitch.
C. Midfield line and center mark:
   i. The pitch is divided widthwise into two halves by a midfield line that joins the midpoints of the two sidelines. The center mark is located at the midpoint of the midfield line.

2.1.2. Pitch dimensions

The dimensions of the pitch shape (See: 2.1.1. Pitch shape) are as follows:

A. Sideline dimensions:
   i. Rectangle vertical length, or sidelines (the distance from keeper zone to keeper zone): 24 yards (22 m).
   ii. Rectangle horizontal width (the width of the midfield line and both keeper zone lines): 36 yards (33 m).
B. Backline dimensions:
   i. Semicircle diameter (the width of the keeper zone lines): 36 yards (33 m).
   ii. Semicircle radius (from the keeper zone line to the backpoint): 18 yards (16.5 m).
C. Additional dimensions:
   i. Pitch vertical length from backpoint to backpoint: 60 yards (55 m).
   ii. Pitch vertical length from hoops to hoops: 36 yards (33 m).

2.1.3. The keeper zone

2.1.3.1. Keeper zone lines—Two lines, which must be marked, connecting the sidelines and parallel to the midfield line. Measuring from the backpoints, these lines are 18 yards (16.5 m) inside the pitch. These lines are 12 yards (11 m) from the midfield line.

2.1.3.2. Extent of the keeper zone—While unmarked off pitch, the keeper zone line extends all the way to the borders of the player area on each side. Each keeper zone extends in the direction of the backpoint on that side of the pitch (away from the midfield line) ending at the boundary of the player area.

2.1.3.3. Own vs. opponents' keeper zone—A team's own keeper zone is the one containing their hoops. A team's opponents' keeper zone is the one containing the hoops through which they are trying to score.

2.1.4. The penalty box

A penalty box must be established for each team. Each penalty box must:

A. Be on the same side of the pitch as the scorekeeper.
B. Be on the same side of the midfield line as the team's bench.
C. The penalty box for each team is located in the player area,

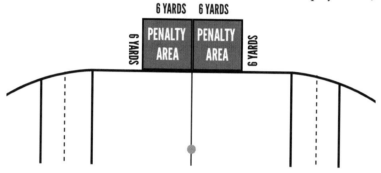

outside of the pitch. The penalty box for each team is a 6 yard by 6 yard (5.5 m by 5.5 m) square area that begins at the midfield line and extends along the pitch sideline in the direction of the team's bench.

See diagram for standard penalty box.

2.1.5. Substitution area and team benches

2.1.5.1. Substitution areas—A substitution area must be established for each team. Each substitution area is an irregular figure with the edge of the pitch as one of its sides, the keeper zone line as one of its sides, and the boundaries of the player area as the other sides. The substitution areas must be part of the player area outside of the pitch boundaries.

A. The following are the boundaries of each substitution area:
   i. The backline of the pitch, within the keeper zone.
   ii. The boundaries of the player area, within the keeper zone except:
   iii. Active substitution should occur outside of the area designated as the team bench.
B. Players within the substitute area:
   i. Players and team staff may leave the team bench and enter the substitute area during the game, but must not remain outside of the team bench.

2.1.5.2. Team benches—The team bench is the space within the substitute area where all players and team staff, except the speaking captain, not in or about to enter active play should be located for the majority of the game.

A. The following people and equipment must remain within the team's bench area:
   i. All substitutes who are not about to enter play or who have exited active play.
   ii. Team staff and coaches, except the speaking captain.
   iii. All of the team's extra equipment, except for additional brooms, which are not allowed in the player area and should be stored at the scorekeeper's table.
B. The team bench is a rectangle of 18 yards (16.5 m) by 3 yards (2.75 m) within each team's substitute area along the same side of the pitch as the scorekeeper table. The following are the boundaries of each team's bench.
   i. An 18 yard (12 m) segment of the player area boundary intersecting the keeper zone line.

ii. An 18 yard (12 m) segment parallel to and 3 yards (2.75 m) away from the boundary of the player area, intersecting the keeper zone line.

iii. A 3 yard (2 m) segment of the keeper zone line.

iv. A 3 yard (2 m) segment connecting the player boundary to the line (ii) above.

C. No benches, tables, or other potentially dangerous or diffi-cult to move obstacles are allowed in the team bench area.

2.1.6. Ball positions

Four ball positions should be indicated directly on the mid-field line.

A. The first two ball positions are 3 yards (2.75 m) on either side of the center mark.

B. The other two ball positions are 9 yards (8.25 m) on either side of the center mark, halfway between the sideline and the center mark.

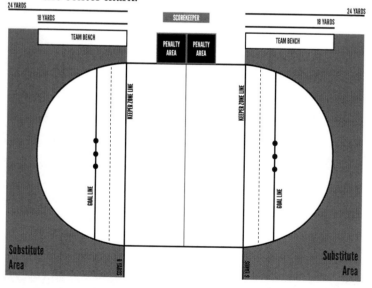

C. These positions may be marked by four small lines that intersect the midfield line called "ball marks."

2.1.7. Additional pitch lines

2.1.7.1. Goal lines—Two lines, which may be marked, that intersect the backlines, parallel to the midfield line.

A. The goal lines are positioned 18 yards (16.5 m) from the midfield line, 12 yards (11 m) from the backpoints, and inside the pitch.
   i. The hoops are positioned along the goal lines, and the hoop positioning must be marked in some manner. These markings must not interfere with the stability of the hoops (See: 2.2.1.3. Hoop positioning).

2.1.7.2. Starting lines—Two lines, which must be marked, parallel to the midfield line, that intersect the sidelines.

A. Each starting line is 3 yards (2.75 m) between a goal line and the closest keeper zone line.

2.1.8. The player and spectator areas

2.1.8.1. The player area—The player area is a rectangle enclosing the pitch with the pitch at its center.

A. This rectangle is:
   i. 48 yards (44 m) wide and 72 yards (66 m) long.
   ii. The midpoint of the pitch is at the center of this area. The midpoint is 24 yards (22 m) and 36 yards (33 m) from the sides of the player area rectangle.
B. The player area must be clear of obstacles and dangerous terrain.

C. During gameplay, the player area is reserved for:
   i. Players and coaches on the active roster of the teams in play.
   ii. Referees and officials assigned to the game currently in play.
   iii. Tournament staff given access to the player area (at their own risk) at the discretion of the head referee or tournament director.

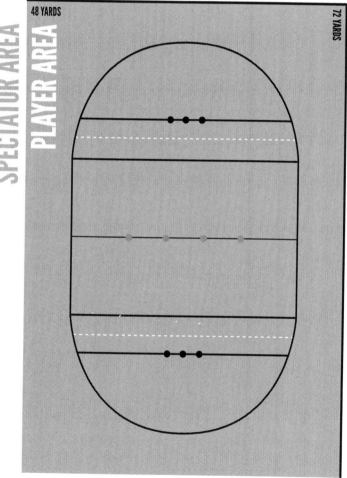

D. No tournament specific obstructions, such as scorekeeping tables, may be set up within the player area.

E. No spectators may enter the player area.

2.1.8.2. The spectator area—Any area outside the player area is the spectator area. Players may never enter the spectator area during a game except in the following circumstances (See: 7.2.5. The spectator area):

A. Players retrieving a game ball with explicit permission of any referee, or if not stopped by a referee while the closest eligible player attempting to retrieve a bludger.

B. Players given explicit permission by the head referee to leave the player area for any other purpose.

C. Players who are in need of medical attention.

D. Players who are assisting another player in need of medical attention.

2.1.9. Field Markings

Various parts of the pitch and surrounding area should be marked in a clear manner. These markings are usually made with cones or lines.

A. The following MUST be marked in some way:
   i. The player area as described in 2.1.8.1.
   ii. The pitch shape as described in 2.1.1.
   iii. The keeper zone lines as described in 2.1.3.1.
   iv. The hoop positioning as described in 2.2.1.3.
   v. The midfield line as described in 2.1.1.C.
   vi. The backpoints as described in 2.1.1.B.
   vii. The starting lines as described in 2.1.7.2.

B. The following markings are optional, though recommend-

ed:
i. The goal lines as described in 2.1.7.1.
ii. The penalty boxes as described in 2.1.4.
iii. The ball marks as described in 2.1.6.
iv. The center mark as described in 2.1.1.C.
v. The team benches as described in 2.1.5.2.
vi. The backlines as described in 2.1.2.B.

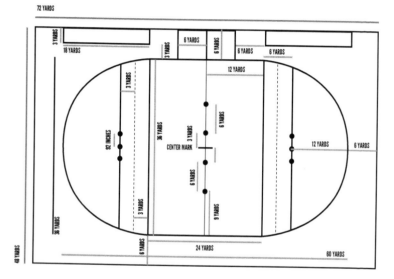

2.2. HOOPS

2.2.1. Specifications

The quidditch hoop is the upright and self supporting structure through which the quaffle must pass to score a goal.

2.2.1.1. Hoop composition and construction

A. Each hoop must be made up of a post and a circular loop attached to the top. These parts of the hoops may be made of any material other than metal or concrete and must not be dangerous to players.

B. A hoop may include a base to keep the hoop upright.
    i. This base should not affect the hoop height.
    ii. Other than metal fasteners, the base must not be made of hard metal or concrete.
C. Hoops must be freestanding and able to withstand play.
    i. Referees must disallow any hoops that they believe are dangerous to the players.

2.2.1.2. Hoop shape

A. Each set of hoops must have posts of three different heights.
    i. These heights must be 3 feet (.91 m), 4.5 feet (1.37m) and 6 feet (1.83 m).
B. A loop must be fastened to the top of each goal post.
    i. The inner diameter of each loop must be between 32 inches and 34 inches (81 cm and 86 cm).
    ii. The attachment of the loop must not make the height of the post exceed the measurements in 2.2.1.2.A.i.

2.2.1.3. Hoop positioning

A. Three hoops are positioned on each goal line.
    i. The 6 foot (1.83 m) hoop must be placed at the center point between the two sidelines parallel with the mid-point on the midfield line.
    ii. The other two hoops are placed 92 inches (7 feet 8 inches, 234 cm) away from the 6 foot (1.83 m) hoop on either side.
    iii. Facing either set of hoops from midfield, the 3 foot (.91m) hoop must be on the left and the 4.5 foot

(1.37m) hoop must be on the right.

2.3. GAME BALLS

2.3.1. The quaffle

Quaffle regulations—The quaffle must be:

A. A spherical ball made of a flexible, smooth leather or leather-like cover of 12 or more panels with a separate bladder (such as a volleyball).

B. Not less than 25.6 inches (65 cm) or more than 26.4 inches (67 cm) in circumference.

C. The quaffle must maintain its spherical shape and must be neither inflated all the way nor so flat that a player could grip a bulk of the leather in one hand.

D. All quaffles used in a game must have the same characteristics regarding circumference, weight, and internal pressure.

E. Any ball specifically approved for play by USQ for use as a quaffle is allowed. Approved quaffles must meet size and inflation guidelines.

2.3.2. Bludgers

Bludger regulations—The three bludgers must be:

A. Spherical balls made of flexible rubber or rubber-like covers (such as dodgeballs).

B. 8.5 inches (22 cm) in diameter, 26.7 inches (68 cm) in circumference.

C. The bludgers must maintain their spherical shape and must be neither inflated all the way nor so flat that a player could grip a bulk of the rubber in one hand.

D. All bludgers used in a game must have the same characteristics regarding circumference, weight, and internal pressure.

E. Any ball specifically approved for play by USQ for use as a bludger is allowed. Approved bludgers must meet size and inflation guidelines.

2.3.3. The snitch

Snitch regulations—The snitch must be:

A. A spherical ball made of a uniform surface consisting of a fabric cover (such as a tennis ball).
B. 8.5 inches (22 cm) in circumference.
C. Held within a sock.
    i. The sock must have a visible and unobstructed length of 10-12 inches (25-31 cm).
    ii. The sock may be tied in a knot or knots, but not to the point that the exposed length is less than 10 inches (25 cm).
D. The sock containing the snitch must be tucked in or attached to the shorts of the snitch runner in a manner that is secure and allows for the removal of the sock by the seeker.

2.4. BROOMS

2.4.1. Broom regulations

The broom:

A. Must consist of a rigid pole made of wood or plastic.
    i. This pole may have "bristles" made of plastic, corn, wood, or other material attached to the back end of the broom. The back of the broom must be to the back

of the player.

    ii. This pole must be between 32 inches (81 cm) and 42 inches (107 cm) long, excluding bristle length.

B. Must not have a total length, including bristles, which exceeds 48 inches (122 cm).

C. Must not have splinters or sharp points.

D. Must not be attached to the body, clothing, or other equipment of the player.

E. Must be allowed if it is specifically approved for play by USQ. Approved brooms must meet length and safety guidelines.

2.4.2. Broken brooms

If a broom breaks during the course of play, the referee must immediately stop play and it must be replaced before its player may make any play.

🏴 *Penalty: Red*—Any player who knowingly initiates a new play of any kind with a broken broom must receive a red card.

2.4.3. Providing brooms

The tournament director for a game is responsible for offering safe brooms of equal length and weight to both teams. Teams may elect to provide their own brooms unless this is disallowed in tournament policy as determined in advance by the tournament director.

2.4.4. Limited brooms in the player area

A. For the first 17 minutes of game time, each team may have a maximum of six brooms within the player area.

B. When the seekers are called to the scorekeeper table at

the 17 minute mark of game time, they will each be given a broom.

   i. After 17 minutes of game time until the game is concluded, each team may have a maximum of seven brooms within the player area.

   ii. All additional brooms, including replacements for broken brooms, must be stored at the scorekeeper table.

2.5. PLAYER EQUIPMENT

2.5.1. Safety

Players must not use any equipment or wear anything that is dangerous to themselves or other players including, but not limited to, any kind of jewelry.

🚩 *Penalty: Red*—Any player who is found to be using illegal equipment that was specifically barred in 2.5. of this rulebook must receive a red card.

2.5.2. Mandatory equipment

While in play, each player must be equipped with the following:

A. A broom.

B. A colored cloth or headband, which must be worn on the forehead, distinguishing the player's position.

   i. The color of the headband must be distinct enough to unambiguously identify the player's position.

   ii. The headband must be thick enough to see easily from a reasonable distance and be identifiable through a player's hair or other equipment.

   iii. Hats or other headwear are not a substitute for headbands, and therefore have no color restrictions. The positional headband must be worn over the headgear and the headband must be clearly distinguishable from the headgear (e.g., the hat and headband may not be the same color).

    a. Exception: If the headwear is both in the shape of a band and is a positional color, it shall be considered a headband. No other positional headband may be worn over this item.

C. A shirt or jersey.

    i. Jerseys for players on the same team must be readily identifiable, of the same base color, and distinguishable from the opposing team.

    ii. Each player must have one of the following distinct numbers, letters or symbols on the back of the player's jersey:

        a. A unique integer between 0 and 999 (a team may have either a 7, a 07, or a 007, but not all three or two of the three).

        b. The symbol for Pi (π), Infinity (∞), or Number (#) (this symbol is also known as pound or hashtag).

        c. One of the following single capital letters: A G H J K M N P R T W X Y

        d. Letters and symbols may not be mixed or combined with integers.

    iii. The primary jersey color may not be yellow or gold.

D. Some sort of bottom (such as shorts, pants, or a skirt). If a player is wearing a skirt, they must also wear shorts or undergarments underneath the skirt.

E. Shoes or cleats (athletic shoes with studs on the bottom).

    i. Spikes or studs must not be sharp.

    ii. Spikes or studs must not be completely made of metal

or affixed with fully metal caps.

F.   A mouthguard which shall:
   i.   Include an occlusal (protecting and separating the biting surfaces) portion.
   ii. Include a labial (protecting the teeth and supporting structures) portion.
   iii. Cover the posterior teeth with adequate thickness.

🏴 *Penalty: Blue*—If a player enters play without one of the above required pieces of equipment, that player must receive a blue card.

🏴 *Penalty: Special*—Illegal Jersey Number: If a team has two players in the player area wearing the same number or symbol after the game starts, or if a player enters play without a legal number on their back, play shall be stopped. The speaking captain shall deem one of their players wearing the offending jersey ineligible to continue play until their jersey is replaced or otherwise modified to read a unique eligible number or symbol. The new number must be reported to the scorekeeper. The speaking captain must receive a blue card. No other penalty shall be given.

🏴 *Penalty: Special*—Illegal headband: If a referee deems a player's headband unacceptable, for any reason, the referee should say "illegal headband." Play is not stopped. The player must leave the pitch and correct the headband or be replaced by a player with a proper headband.

🏴 *Penalty: Yellow*—Any player who ignores the directive "illegal headband" or makes a play after being given the directive must receive a yellow card.

2.5.3. Additional equipment

A. Padding—All padding must:
  i. Be one inch or less in thickness.
  ii. Pass the "knock test," i.e. when a referee raps on it with a knuckle, it should not make a knocking sound.
  iii. Bend easily when a minimal amount of force is applied to it.
B. Braces—Athletic braces are allowed but must generally meet the standards of padding above.
  i. A brace may include a hard element; however, any hard plastic or metal in a brace must be covered at all times during a game and, once covered, must pass the referee "knock test."
  ii. If any hard plastic or metal becomes exposed, the player must leave the pitch and fix the problem (See: 2.5.4. Accidental infringement of equipment rules).
  iii. Referees reserve the right to refuse any brace that they believe presents a danger to the players.
C. Athletic supporters—Athletic supporters (cups) which are used used to protect the groin are allowed.
D. Glasses and eyewear—Players may wear glasses or other eyewear, such as goggles.
  i. No eyewear actually made of glass will be allowed unless it is worn underneath goggles so the glass is not exposed.
  ii. Goggles made of metal, such as lacrosse "cage" goggles are not allowed.
E. Gloves—Gloves are allowed.
F. Hand or glove grip enhancers—Hand and glove grip enhancing substances which might transfer to and affect a ball are illegal.
G. Special equipment—Individuals with disabilities or recovering from injuries may require other specific equipment.

Such equipment must be approved by USQ via USQ's equipment waiver policy prior to its use in any official game.

H. Any additional equipment must be approved by the head referee before the game. Any equipment that the referee determines to be dangerous or unfair to either team must not be permitted.

🏴 *Penalty: Blue*—A player who is found to be using illegal equipment after the game has started must receive a blue card. This does not include equipment that breaks or is otherwise altered due to the course of play.

🏴 *Penalty: Red*—A player who is found to be using illegal equipment that was specifically barred by the referee or tournament director before the game began, during ground rules, or at any previous point during the game must receive a red card.

2.5.4. Accidental infringement of equipment rules

In the event of any accidental infringement of the equipment rules:

A. Play is not stopped unless the referee determines the infringement presents a danger to players.

B. The player at fault must leave the pitch to correct the equipment immediately and may be replaced with a substitute.

C. Any player required to leave the pitch to correct equipment must not reenter until the equipment has been replaced or repaired.

D. If there is no replacement for mandatory equipment available, the referee must stop play until the equipment is provided.

🚩 *Penalty: Yellow*—A player who has been required to leave the pitch because of an equipment infringement and who reenters without correcting the infringement must receive a yellow card.

2.5.5. Intentionally altering equipment

It is illegal to intentionally alter any game equipment, including the game balls and hoops, so that it does not match the regulations in the rules.

🚩 *Penalty: Red*—A player who intentionally alters any equipment in order to gain an advantage must receive a red card.

2.5.6. Headband lost mid-play

If a player's headband is lost mid-play, they may remain in play until they are either knocked out, there is a stoppage in play, or a goal is scored, but the player must replace the headband as soon as possible. Seekers do not have to replace their headband when a goal is scored, but the other two requirements apply.

🚩 *Penalty: Back to hoops*—A player who does not replace a lost headband when knocked out, at a stoppage of play, or when a goal is scored must be sent back to hoops and must replace the headband before reentering play.

2.5.7. Damaged jersey number

If a player's number becomes damaged beyond recognition during play:

A. Play is not stopped.
B. The referee must inform the player that their jersey number

has been damaged.

C. The player must fix the number the next time they substitute out of the game, or during the next stoppage in play, whichever occurs first.

    i. If there is a stoppage in play, and the number cannot be quickly fixed, the player may substitute out during that stoppage.

    ii. If the issue can only be addressed by giving the player a new number, that new number must be reported to the scorekeeper.

D. If the player substitutes back in without fixing the number, or remains in the game with the damaged number after the next stoppage, the damaged number shall be treated as an illegal jersey number (See: 2.5.2. Mandatory equipment).

3. Game Procedures

3.1. PRELIMINARIES

3.1.1. Pregame meeting

Before any game, the head referee calls together the two teams to go over general rules.

A. Each team must designate one person to serve as speaking captain to represent the team during the game.
   i. The speaking captain is the only person who may speak on behalf of the team to any referee or official with regard to the game.
   ii. The speaking captain may be a player or non-player, but must be on the team's official roster. A team's coach may serve as the speaking captain.
   iii. Any official team captains (including the speaking captain) and coaches may attend the pregame meeting, but the team must clearly indicate which individual is the speaking captain for the game.
B. At this time, the head referee and snitch runner should ensure that each team is clear on the following:
   i. Any ground rules specific to the field.
   ii. Any and all planned snitch spectacles.
   iii. Any rules changes or clarifications that may impact the game.
   iv. Any special considerations for a team's players that the

referee should know regarding the gender maximum rule (See: 7.1.3. Gender maximum rule).

v. Any other concerns from the attending parties that are specific to the game.

3.1.2. Coin toss

Teams may elect to have a coin toss to determine which team will attack which set of hoops.

A. If either team requests a coin toss, the head referee and opposing team must accommodate the request.

B. The toss shall be called while the coin is in the air by:
   i. The team with the lower USQ ranking.
   ii. If the ranking is inapplicable or unknown, the team that has traveled farthest from its point of origin shall call the toss.

C. The team that wins the coin toss selects which set of hoops it will attack for the duration of regulation time (for overtime procedures, see: 3.5. Overtime).

3.2. STARTING THE GAME

3.2.1. Pregame lineup and procedure

In order to begin the game:

A. The six starters on each team must line up on the pitch behind the starting line.
   i. Each team must start the game with three chasers, one keeper, and two beaters.
   ii. Players may line up in any order.
   iii. All players must remain behind the starting line (See: 2.1.7.2. Starting lines).

    iv. Players may change position until the head referee shouts "Brooms Down!"

    v. Any player who receives a card prior to the start of the game (or their substitute in the case of a red) must start the game in the penalty box.

B. All balls (excluding the snitch) must be resting in the appropriate positions (See: 2.1.6. Ball positions).

    i. The quaffle must be placed at one of the two ball positions closest to the midpoint of the pitch.

    ii. Any ball (excluding the snitch) which moves, for any reason, must be reset before the head referee calls "Brooms Up!"

C. The head referee confirms that both teams, all assistant referees, and any other officials are ready and identifies the snitch runner.

    i. The snitch runner must not be in the player area at the start of the game.

    ii. The snitch runner must report to the scorekeeper by the 17 minute mark of game time to be released into the player area in anticipation of the seeker release at the 18 minute mark (See: 3.4.1.2. Seeker floor).

D. The head referee shouts "Brooms Down!"

E. Once "Brooms Down!" has been called:

    i. Players may not change position on the starting line.

    ii. No part of a player's body may contact the ground in front of the starting line.

    iii. Each player must have a broom in hand.

        a. The broom must remain otherwise flat on the ground until "Brooms Up!" is called.

F. The head referee shouts "Ready!"

    i. Players may assume a starting position at the call of

"ready," but in doing so the broom must remain flat on the ground.

G. A few seconds after the head referee shouts "Ready!" the referee then shouts "Brooms Up!"

    i. On the first "B" sound of "Brooms Up!" all players must immediately mount their brooms and begin play.

    ii. If there is a false call of "Brooms Up!" the head referee resets the players and repeats the procedure of 3.2.1.

    iii. In the event of any penalty prior to "Brooms Up!", the referee adjudicates the penalty and then resets the players and repeats the procedure of 3.2.1.

⚑ *Penalty: Blue*—A player who changes position on the starting line after the referee has called "Brooms Down!" must receive a blue card.

⚑ *Penalty: Blue*—If a player picks up their broom, but is able to reset with their broom flat on the ground before the referee calls "Brooms Up!", then play may continue as "No harm, no foul." If a player has not reset before the the first "B" sound of "Brooms Up!" or if a player moves early and touches the ground on the other side of the starting line prior to the call of "Brooms Up!," that player must receive a blue card and the referee must reset the other players and repeat the procedure of 3.2.1.

3.3. STOPPING PLAY

3.3.1. Stopping play procedure

To stop play:

A. The referee blows a whistle in paired short blasts.

B. The timekeeper stops the game time.

C. All players currently in play must stop, drop their brooms, and hold their respective positions.

    i. The players maintain any balls they possessed and may not pick up any balls during the stoppage.

        a. Any balls not possessed must be left on the ground, except in the situation described in 3.3.1.J.ii.a.

    ii. Any players who are paused in an illegal position are adjusted immediately to a legal position.

    iii. Any players who accidentally (and significantly) moved after the whistle are returned to their location at the time the whistle was blown.

D. The head referee consults with other referees as necessary concerning:

    i. The adjudication of fouls.

    ii. The legality of any snitch catch. If a legal snitch catch occurred, the game ends or proceeds to an overtime period as appropriate (See: 3.4.2. Ending the game).

    iii. Any other relevant concerns.

E. The referee adjudicates any fouls and communicates the type of foul to the players, scorekeeper, and spectators:

    i. Any players who have committed back to hoops offenses are informed that they must return to their hoops upon resumption of play (See: 9.1.1. Back to hoops fouls).

    ii. Any players who committed a blue card offense or their first yellow card offense are sent to the penalty box, while ensuring that each team has a keeper in play (See: 9.1.3. Blue card and 9.1.4. Yellow card).

    iii. Any players who have committed a red card offense are sent off and their substitute is sent to the penalty box, while ensuring that each team has a keeper in play (See: 9.1.5. Red card).

F. If a change of possession occurs:
   i. In the quaffle game:
      a. The quaffle is given to the chaser or keeper from the appropriate team who is nearest the quaffle.
   ii. In the bludger game:
      a. If the team to receive possession has no bludgers or only one bludger, the bludger is given to the beater from that team who is nearest the bludger in question.
      b. If the team to receive possession has two bludgers, the bludger must remain where it was at the stoppage of play.
         1. If the player holding the ball is sent to the penalty box, the ball must be placed on the ground where they were standing at the time of the stoppage.
G. Any players who are injured are replaced.
H. Any external interference is removed.
I. Any defective equipment is fixed, replaced, or removed (if the equipment was not mandatory).
J. The referee indicates to the players that play is about to resume by calling for the players to "Remount!"
   i. Players must remount their brooms at the same location where the brooms were left when play was stopped.
   ii. Players must stand at the call to remount.
      a. If two players on the ground each had a grip on a ball when play was stopped, they still must stand. Once standing, each may retake hold of that ball. They do not need to hold it in the same way they had on the ground.
         1. Whether a player is considered to have had a grip on a ball is determined by the status at the

moment play was stopped.

K. The referee blows one short whistle blast. On this whistle blast:

    i. Play resumes.

    ii. The timekeeper resumes the game time, and all other time clocks.

🏴 *Penalty: Yellow*—Any player who continues to move intentionally or refuses a referee's instructions to return to their position at the time of a stoppage must receive a yellow card.

🏴 *Penalty: Yellow*—Any player who illegally picks up or otherwise takes hold of a ball during a stoppage, with the intent to deceive an official into believing they had hold of that ball prior to the stoppage, must receive a yellow card.

3.3.2. Head referee stopping play

The head referee stops play using the procedure described in 3.3.1. in any of the following circumstances:

A. A player commits a foul that results in a change of quaffle possession.

B. A player commits a foul that results in a blue card, yellow card, or red card.

C. The referee is unsure of a call and needs to consult with the other referees.

D. A player is too injured to continue play while obstructing active gameplay or is down with a serious injury.

E. An external interference occurs, including when a ball or player from another pitch enters the pitch.

F. A ball becomes defective (See: 3.3.7. Defective balls mid-play).

G. If there is a broken broom anywhere within the player area.

H. A hoop is broken in a way that:

    i. Presents a danger to players.

    ii. Cannot be easily fixed and:

        a. Is not near active gameplay.

        b. Is not being attacked by an offense which has already crossed the midfield line with the quaffle (See: 4.2. Broken or fallen hoops).

I. All three hoops on one side fall down or become defective (See: 4.2. Broken or fallen hoops).

J. Quaffle play moves too close to dangerous terrain or spectators (See: 7.2.6. Spectators and dangerous terrain).

K. A player commits a foul that would otherwise not stop play, but the player does not respond to the referee's call.

L. An assistant referee sees a foul against or committed by the quaffle carrier, which the head referee is unlikely to have seen, and the stoppage of play would not create an advantage for the fouling team. Stopping play in this circumstance is at the discretion of the head referee.

3.3.3. Snitch referee stopping play

The snitch referee stops play using the procedure in 3.3.1. in any of the following circumstances.

A. The snitch referee believes that a snitch catch is good.

B. The snitch runner is injured or needs to be replaced.

C. The snitch ball or snitch shorts become defective and need to be replaced.

3.3.4. Advantage

If the head referee determines that stopping play due to a foul would provide an advantage to the fouling team, the referee may call advantage by raising one hand straight into the air.

3.3.4.1. Calling advantage:

A. If advantage is called the following procedure applies:
   i. The referee throws a marker indicating the location of the quaffle at the time of the foul.
   ii. The referee may send the fouling player back to hoops at the start of the advantage if the situation warrants.
   iii. Play continues until the fouling team would no longer benefit from play being stopped including, but not limited to, the following situations:
       a. The fouling team gains possession of the quaffle.
       b. A goal is scored for the fouled team.
       c. A goal is scored for the fouling team; this goal is disallowed.
       d. The fouled team commits a separate foul.
       e. There is a snitch catch by either team.
          1. If the fouling team catches the snitch during advantage, then the catch must be called no good and the referee should adjudicate the penalty and restart play.
          2. If the fouled team catches the snitch during advantage and the catch is otherwise good, then the catch must be called good and the referee should declare the period over. All fouls should still be listed on the official scorecard.
B. If a foul is committed involving only the seekers or a seeker and the snitch runner, advantage should not be called.
   i. For such fouls resulting in a card, the procedure found in rule 3.3.5.3.B. should be applied.

3.3.4.2. When advantage abates, the referee must stop play and perform the following actions:

A. If a goal is scored for the fouled team, the goal must be called good and:

   i. If advantage was called on a back to hoops offense, then the standard procedure for back to hoops is applied. Generally, advantage should not be called on a back to hoops offense.

   ii. If the foul results in a blue card or a yellow card and the fouling team's penalty box is empty, the penalty time is nullified by the score.

   iii. If the foul results in a blue or yellow card and a player from the fouling team is in the penalty box serving time for a blue or yellow card, the player with the least remaining penalty time is released and the fouling player is sent to the penalty box for one minute or until the fouled team scores.

   iv. If the foul results in a blue card or a yellow card and the only player in the fouling team's penalty box is a substitute serving time for a red card, then the penalty time for the player receiving the blue or yellow card is nullified by the score.

   v. If the foul results in a red card, the fouling player's substitute is sent to the penalty box for two minutes.

B. If the advantage of stopping play for the fouling team abates in any way other than a goal, then the referee stops play immediately and applies the appropriate penalty for all fouls.

   i. If a player on the fouled team commits a foul during advantage, this foul ends the advantage and is adjudicated in the same manner as a foul in any other circumstance.

  a. If both teams have committed fouls which would turn over the same ball, possession of that ball is determined by:

    1. The foul receiving the most severe card.

    2. If multiple fouls receive the most severe card, or lack thereof, among those fouls, the foul committed last.

    3. For the purpose of determining possession under this rule, turnovers from the advantage restart procedure shall be considered part of the penalty for which the advantage was initially called.

  ii. If a player on the fouling team, other than the original fouling player, commits a separate foul during advantage, the referee may decide to stop play or continue advantage as appropriate.

    a. Both penalties must be adjudicated regardless of whether advantage continues.

  iii. If the player who committed the original foul commits a second foul during advantage, the referee may decide to stop play or continue advantage as appropriate.

    a. If the referee believes that the fouling player intentionally committed the second foul, the penalties for both fouls must be given.

    b. If the referee believes the fouling player did not intentionally commit the second foul, the penalty for the more egregious of the two fouls is given.

3.3.4.3. Snitch catches during advantage:

A. Any snitch catch by the fouling team during advantage

must be called no good.

B. Any snitch catch by the fouled team that meets the criteria for a good catch must be called good.

   i. If the foul results in a blue card or a yellow card and the fouling team's penalty box was empty at the time of the catch, the penalty time is nullified by the score.

3.3.4.4. Restart procedure after advantage has been called:

A. If a goal is scored for the fouled team:

   i. If advantage was called due to a foul in the quaffle game, then play restarts according to standard procedure for a goal (See: 4.4. Restarting after a goal).

   ii. If advantage was called due to a foul in the bludger game:

      a. If the fouling team retained possession of two bludgers at the end of advantage, the bludger possessed by the beater who committed the foul is given to the nearest eligible beater from the opposing team.

      b. All other plays made by beaters or changes in bludger possession for either team during the advantage are valid.

   iii. If advantage was called due to a foul by a seeker, then play restarts according to the standard procedure for a goal (See: 4.4. Restarting after a goal).

B. If advantage was called due to a foul in the quaffle game and the fouled team did not score:

   i. The quaffle carrier at the time of the foul (or their substitute) is returned to the location of the advantage marker before play is resumed.

      a. If this player has been knocked out, they are returned to the location of the advantage marker as an eligible player, even if they have not completed the knockout procedure.

b. The quaffle is returned to this player.

c. If this player committed a back to hoops foul during the advantage, other than dismounting, or has been sent to the penalty box, the quaffle player from that team, nearest to the advantage marker, shall move to the location of the advantage marker and receive the quaffle instead.

d. If, under 3.3.4.2.B.i.a., the quaffle is turned over to the originally fouling team, no players shall be moved to the location of the advantage marker.

ii. All other players remain where they were at the time of the stoppage and, if knocked out before the stoppage, continue to be knocked out and must follow the knockout procedure as outlined in 5.3.1. Knockout procedure.

C. If advantage was called due to a foul in the bludger game and the fouled team did not score:

i. Quaffle play is reset as outlined in 3.3.4.4.B.i.

ii. If the fouling team retained possession of two bludgers during the advantage, the bludger possessed by the beater who committed the foul is given to the nearest eligible opposing beater at the time of the stoppage.

iii. All other plays made by beaters or changes in bludger possession for either team during the advantage are valid.

D. Play is resumed by the head referee.

3.3.5. Delayed penalties

All blue, yellow, and red card penalties called by officials other than the head referee are considered delayed penalties because of the time between the offense and when the head referee is able to stop play and adjudicate the penalty.

3.3.5.1. Calling a delayed penalty:

A. If an official other than the head referee sees a player or coach commit a foul, that official raises their hand and play continues as a delayed penalty.

    i. If the penalty is back to hoops or a turnover, the official may adjudicate the penalty while play continues rather than using this procedure.

B. The assistant referee may send the fouling player back to hoops during the delay if the situation warrants.

C. The referee visually and verbally signals to the head referee that a foul has occurred and which team committed the foul.

    i. If the head referee determines that it is appropriate to immediately stop play, the head referee may do so.

    ii. The head referee may allow play continue as in an advantage situation until the advantage abates in any way, unless the foul continues or escalates.

        a. If the head referee continues play as in an advantage situation, they shall raise their own arm as well.

D. If another foul is committed during a delayed penalty, by either team, the head referee should stop play and adjudicate both fouls immediately.

    i. If both teams have committed fouls which would turn over the same ball, possession of that ball is determined by:

        a. The foul receiving the most severe card.

        b. If multiple fouls receive the same card, or lack thereof, among those fouls, the foul committed last.

    c. For the purpose of this determining possession under this rule, turnovers from the delayed penalty procedure shall be considered part of the penalty for which the delay was initially called.

  ii. If the originally fouling player commits a second foul during the delay, and the referee believes the fouling player did not intentionally commit the second foul, that player shall only receive the penalty for the more egregious of those two offenses.

E. If called due to a foul by a seeker, follow the procedure in 3.3.5.3.

3.3.5.2. Except in the situation described in 3.3.5.3.B., when the referee stops play for a delayed penalty:

A. If the fouling team scored a goal during the delay, the goal is discounted, whether or not the foul directly affected the goal. The defending keeper receives possession of the quaffle in their own keeper zone.

B. If neither team scored during the delay:

  i. On a yellow or red card foul, the quaffle is turned over to the closest eligible player of the fouled team, whether or not the foul directly affected possession.

  ii. On a blue card foul, the quaffle is turned over to the closest eligible player of the fouled team if the foul resulted in a change of quaffle possession, or the fouled team lost the quaffle during the delay.

C. If the fouled team scores, standard advantage procedure should be implemented (See: 3.3.4.4.A.).

D. After all penalties are adjudicated, play is restarted.

3.3.5.3. Delayed seeker penalties

A. If a seeker commits a blue, yellow, or red card offense in or as a result of an interaction with any player other than the opposing seeker or the snitch runner, it shall be called immediately, or follow the procedures listed in 3.3.4. (Advantage) or 3.3.5.1.A-D. and 3.3.5.2. (Delayed Penalty) as appropriate.

B. If a seeker commits a blue, yellow, or red card offense in or as a result of an interaction involving no players other than the opposing seeker or the snitch runner, regardless of which referee is making the call, and the following procedure shall be followed.

   i. Play continues as a delayed penalty.

   ii. The referee may send the fouling seeker back to hoops as the situation warrants.

   iii. If this referee is not the head referee, the referee visually and verbally signals to the head referee that a foul has occurred and that it is a seeker foul.

   iv. The head referee shall allow play to continue until a goal is scored or stopping play would not disadvantage either team.

      a. If the same seeker commits another foul during the delay, play must be stopped.

         1. If the referee believes that the fouling player intentionally committed the second foul, the penalties for both fouls must be given.

         2. If the referee believes the fouling player did not intentionally commit the second foul, the penalty for the more egregious of the two fouls is given.

         3. If the later foul involved a player other than the

opposing seeker or snitch runner, 3.3.5.3.B.v.a-b does not apply.

    b. If any other player commits another foul during this delay, the proper procedure for stopping play for that penalty shall be followed instead.

v. The penalty is adjudicated.

    a. No turnovers shall be enforced as a result of the seeker's penalty.

        1. This includes the turnovers listed in the penalty card procedure sections (See: 9.1.3-5).

    b. No goals shall be disallowed as a result of the seeker's penalty.

vi. Play is restarted.

3.3.5.4. Snitch catches during delayed penalties:

A. Any snitch catch by the fouling team during a delayed penalty must be called no good and the snitch is reset.

B. Any snitch catch by the non-fouling team during a delayed penalty, that is otherwise good, must be called good.

3.3.6. Delay of game

3.3.6.1. Delay of game—Delay of game is defined as an attempt to stop or significantly impede the quaffle game from continuing. The exact determination of what constitutes delay of game is at the discretion of the referee, within the following guidelines:

A. The following scenarios, and any that can reasonably be considered fitting in the same categories, should not be considered delay of game:

    i. After moving forward to attack, the offense passes backwards to a quaffle player, including resetting the quaffle to a quaffle player in the keeper zone. Though not technically "advancing" the quaffle, the play allows the offense to set up strategically and gameplay is not affected.

ii. The quaffle carrier is forced to stop by the defense or is on the ground and unable to continue moving.

iii. The quaffle carrier moves slowly but consistently up the pitch with the ball.

iv. A beater or beaters are guarding the quaffle that is still on the ground and their team's quaffle players are making a reasonable effort to gain possession and restart quaffle play.

B. The following scenarios, and others that can be reasonably considered fitting in the same categories, should be considered delay of game in most circumstances:

i. The offense moves forward with the ball and stops moving completely or takes extreme measures to move slowly or erratically, without being forced to do so by the defense, including, but not limited to:

a. The quaffle carrier stands stationary behind a beater in possession of a bludger.

b. The quaffle carrier tiptoes or zigzags slowly up the pitch.

c. Players repeatedly toss the quaffle between two players on their own side of the midfield line.

ii. A beater or beaters guard the quaffle that is still on the ground, but their team's quaffle players are not making a reasonable effort to gain possession of the quaffle and restart quaffle play.

iii. A player carries the quaffle to the vicinity of the sideline while substituting out.

      a. This shall not be considered delay of game if all other quaffle players on the player's team are in the penalty box.

C. Keeper delay:

    i. A protected keeper must directly and immediately advance the quaffle out of the keeper zone, attempt to complete a pass, or drop the quaffle to the ground.

    ii. After a goal, the keeper on the formerly defensive team must not substitute out of the game until they have gained possession of the quaffle and made it live.

🚩 *Penalty: Warning*—The head referee may issue a warning when the referee determines that the team is beginning to delay the game. Teams must respond immediately to this warning or incur further penalty. Multiple warnings may be given for delay of game during a single game, as the referee determines to be appropriate.

🚩 *Penalty: Blue*—A player who the head referee determines to be delaying the game may receive a blue card. If the blue card is issued, the quaffle must be turned over to the closest eligible player of the opposing team to the point of the foul. A warning does not need to be given prior to issuing the blue card if the referee determines that the infraction alone was significant enough to warrant the blue card.

3.3.6.2. Resetting—A team may not reset the quaffle into their own half, or further away from the midfield line within their own half, without either attempting a pass to an eligible receiver or attempting to score a goal through their opponents' hoops, at the discretion of the referee.

A. A receiver's eligibility is determined at the arrival of the quaffle, not the time of the pass.

B. Resetting only applies if the quaffle is propelled in a manner that can reasonably be considered a "reset" at the discretion of the referee.

C. Resetting does not apply to loose balls, unless a player intentionally made the quaffle loose in order for their team to attempt a reset.

🏳 *Penalty: Turnover*—If a player resets illegally, then play shall be stopped and the quaffle shall be given to the closest eligible player on the opposing team at the point from which the fouling player reset the quaffle. Even if the position to which the ball was moved by the reset is advantageous to the non-fouling team, the head referee must not exercise the option to turn over the ball at the new location, but may choose to call no harm no foul, if appropriate, and allow play to continue.

3.3.7. Defective balls mid-play

If a game ball becomes defective (deflates, etc.) while in play, the head referee must stop play to replace the ball. The following conditions apply:

A. The head referee must stop play immediately when any ball becomes defective.

  i. There is no advantage for either team when a ball becomes defective and where the ball is located on the pitch is irrelevant.

  ii. All assistant referees should immediately inform the head referee of a defective ball.

B. If a ball was in midair when it became defective, the replaced or repaired ball is returned to the player who last held possession, except the quaffle after a good goal.

C. No goals, knockouts, or snitch catches may happen with a defective ball.

D. If the quaffle becomes defective while going through a hoop, no goal is scored unless the quaffle had already passed entirely through the hoop before becoming defective.

E. If a bludger becomes defective while hitting a player:

   i. The knockout counts.

   ii. When a beater is struck, that beater may still catch the defective bludger to negate the knockout.

      a. If a live bludger becomes defective by sticking on the end of an opponent's broom, the opponent is knocked out. This action is not considered to be a catch.

F. If the snitch ball becomes defective during the snitch catch (eg. the sock breaks in half and the seeker gets half of it):

   i. The catch counts if the seeker cleanly removed the actual ball.

   ii. If the snitch ball becomes defective before the catch, the catch must be called no good.

   iii. The snitch referee should stop play if the snitch cannot be easily repaired.

   iv. The replaced or repaired snitch ball is refastened to the snitch runner and play continues.

3.4. REGULATING GAME TIME

3.4.1. Game length

3.4.1.1. Game time—Game time is measured in real time beginning from the first "B" sound in the head referee's call of

"Brooms Up!"

   A. The game time, and any time associated with it, must be paused for all complete stoppages of play and resumed when play is resumed.

      i. All clocks should be paused at any time a referee's whistle is blown in short paired blasts to stop play.

      ii. All clocks should be restarted on the head referee's short whistle blast to resume play.

   B. There may be no rule or regulation strictly defining the length of a game.

3.4.1.2. Seeker floor—The seeker floors are the first 18 minutes of game time during regulation time, and the first 30 seconds of the first overtime, during which the snitch may not be caught.

   A. Seeker floors must be measured in game time.

   B. During a seeker floor, there are no seekers in play.

   C. A seeker from each team should report to the timekeeper at or before the 17 minute mark of game time in regulation.

      i. Seekers are not eligible to interact with play in any way until they are released by the timekeeper.

      ii. Seekers must remain within the penalty box until being released by the timekeeper.

      iii. There is no penalty for failing to report to the time-keeper prior to the 17 minute mark of game time. However each team's initial seeker must check in with the timekeeper and be released into the game from the penalty box, even if this occurs after the end of the seeker floor.

         a. If the initial seeker checks in after the end of the seeker floor, the timekeeper shall provide the seeker with a broom and release them into the game immediately upon confirming that they are mounted on the broom in the penalty box.

D. The snitch runner may enter the player area at any time after the 17 minute mark of game time and must have entered prior to the 18 minute mark of game time.

E. At the end of the seeker floor, the timekeeper releases the seekers from their respective penalty boxes to pursue the snitch runner (See: 7.5. Seeker rules).

🏳 *Penalty: Blue* —If a seeker leaves the penalty box before the end of the seeker floor, they must receive a blue card. Penalty time shall begin at the end of the seeker floor for that period, and the player must serve the time as a seeker.

🏳 *Penalty: Blue*—If a team's initial seeker for the period enters the game without checking in with the timekeeper and being released from the penalty box, that player must receive a blue card. If this occurs prior to the end of the seeker floor, the penalty time shall begin at the end of the seeker floor for that period, and the player must serve the time as a seeker.

3.4.1.3. Snitch handicaps

A. The following handicaps on the snitch runner are cumulative and must be implemented in all games at their assigned times as measured in game time.

  i. Upon the release of the seekers, the snitch runner is required to remain between the keeper zone lines.

  ii. At the 23 minute mark of game time, the snitch runner is required to remain within roughly 1.5 yards of the midline of the field.

    iii. At the 28 minute mark of game time, the snitch runner is required to use only one arm.

    iv. At the 33 minute mark of game time, the snitch runner is required to remain within roughly 1.5 yards of the intersection of the midline of the pitch and sideline of the pitch opposite the scorekeeper and benches.

B. Snitch runners may choose to further handicap themselves during a game, however tournament staff and game officials must neither order nor request that they do so.

C. No snitch catch shall be invalidated due to a snitch runner not being in compliance with the handicaps.

D. Repeated violations of the handicaps is grounds for the replacement of the snitch runner.

E. If a game proceeds to overtime, all handicaps on the snitch runner are removed for the remainder of the game, except for the requirement to remain between the keeper zone lines, and no further handicaps shall be implemented.

3.4.2. Ending the game

3.4.2.1. Ending regulation time:

A. The head referee or snitch referee shall stop play by blowing a whistle in paired short blasts when either believes a good snitch catch may have occurred (See: 4.5. The snitch catch).

    i. After play is stopped, the head referee should check verbally or visually with all relevant assistant referees to ensure there are no legitimate challenges to the validity of the catch.

        a. In the case of any disagreement between officials, the head referee makes the final decision as to the status of the catch.

ii. If the snitch catch was no good, the snitch must be reset and play restarted.

iii. If the snitch catch was good, the head referee shall blow three long whistle blasts to indicate the end of the period.

B. If the game is not tied, the game ends and the team with the most total points is declared the winner.

C. If the game is tied, the game proceeds to overtime (See: 3.5.2. First overtime).

3.4.2.2. Ending first overtime—There are two ways that a first overtime period may end:

A. If the entire five minutes of game time passes without a clean snitch catch, the head referee must blow three long whistle blasts, indicating the end of the period.

i. If the game is not tied, the game ends and the team with the most total points is declared the winner.

ii. If the game is tied, the game proceeds to a sudden death second overtime (See: 3.5.3. Second overtime).

B. If the snitch has been caught cleanly in overtime, the head referee must blow three long whistle blasts indicating the end of the period.

i. If the game is not tied, the game ends and the team with the most total points is declared the winner.

ii. If the game is tied, the game proceeds to second overtime (See: 3.5.3. Second overtime).

3.4.2.3. Ending second overtime—Second overtime ends immediately following any score by either team.

A. If the snitch has been caught cleanly in second overtime, the head referee must blow three long whistle blasts indicating the end of the period and game.

B. Upon confirming a good goal by either team in second overtime, the head referee must also blow three long whistle blasts indicating the end of the period and game.

3.5. OVERTIME

3.5.1. Going to overtime

In a situation where both teams have scored an equal amount of points after the snitch has been caught in regulation time, the game proceeds into overtime.

3.5.2. First overtime

The following procedure is observed for the first overtime period:

A. The two teams switch ends of the pitch that they are defending.

B. The referees reset the pitch.

C. The head referee must grant the teams approximately 3 minutes of rest between regulation time and overtime.

D. At the call of the referee, both teams take their positions at the starting line.

    i. If there are players serving time in the penalty box for a blue or yellow card, the snitch catch that ended regulation time is treated as a single score for the purposes of releasing a player. All other players must serve the remainder of their penalty time during the first overtime period.

E. The referee begins play by following the procedure in 3.2.

Starting the game.

F. The snitch must enter the pitch at some point between the start of the period and the 30 second mark of overtime.

G. A 30-second seeker floor applies before seekers may pursue the snitch.

  i. Prior to the "brooms up" call of overtime, the seekers should check in with the timekeeper to be released from the penalty box when the 30 second seeker floor has concluded.

  ii. At the end of the 30 seconds, the seekers are released to pursue the snitch.

  iii. There is no penalty for failing to report to the timekeeper prior to start of overtime. However each team's initial seeker in overtime must check in with the timekeeper and be released into the game from the penalty box, even if this occurs after the 30 second mark of overtime.

   a. If the initial seeker checks in after the 30 second mark, the timekeeper shall provide the seeker with a broom and release them into the game immediately upon confirming that they are mounted on the broom in the penalty box.

  iv. If a seeker's penalty time extends into the first overtime, the seeker's penalty clock will not run until the seeker floor has ended, and no scores during the seeker floor can release the seeker.

   a. The seeker remains ineligible to play at any position during the seeker floor.

H. Overtime lasts five minutes of game time or until the snitch has been legally caught. After either has occurred, the team with the higher score is declared the winner.

I. Timekeeper role in overtime:

    i. The timekeeper must announce each minute time has passed in overtime (4, 3, 2, 1).

    ii. The timekeeper must announce 30 seconds and 15 seconds remaining.

    iii. The timekeeper must count down from 10.

    iv. If a referee makes an advantage or delayed penalty call during first overtime, the timekeeper must stop the overtime clock as soon as the head referee's arm is raised or their advantage marker is thrown. The overtime clock must remain stopped until the foul is resolved. This way, a team may not attempt to run out the overtime clock by intentionally fouling.

J. If both teams have scored an equal amount of points after first overtime, the game proceeds into second overtime.

3.5.3. Second overtime

In a situation where both teams have scored an equal amount of points after the first overtime, the game proceeds into a sudden death second overtime. The following procedure is observed for the second overtime period:

A. Teams do not switch ends of the pitch before the second overtime.

B. The referees reset the pitch and players immediately.

    i. If there are players serving time in the penalty box for a blue or yellow card, the snitch catch that ended first overtime (unless ended by expiration of time) is treated as a single score for the purposes of releasing a player. All other players must serve the remainder of their penalty time during the second overtime period.

C. The referee begins play by following the procedure in 3.2.

Starting the game.

D. The snitch must remain on the midfield line until "Brooms Up!" is called.

E. There is no seeker floor in second overtime. The seekers must start the period on the starting line.

F. The first team to score any points, by quaffle or by snitch, is declared the winner.

3.6. FORFEITS & SUSPENDED GAMES

3.6.1. Forfeits

3.6.1.1. Declaring a game a forfeit:

A. The head referee may declare a game forfeit due to the speaking captain of a team officially requesting a forfeit.

B. The head referee may declare a game forfeit if any player persists in refusing to leave after receiving a red card or becomes a danger to spectators, players, or officials.

C. The head referee may declare a game forfeit if a team has less than four remaining eligible players (including those in the penalty box).

D. A game may be declared forfeit due to violations of league or tournament policy.

3.6.1.2. In the event of a forfeit:

A. The game is over immediately and the forfeiting team is declared the losing team.

B. All players should clear the field to discourage any potential escalation.

3.6.2. Suspended games

3.6.2.1. Declaring a suspended game:

A. The head referee or tournament director may declare a game suspended due to weather, safety concerns, extreme or inappropriate misconduct, or external interference.

B. Suspended games must be recorded with the current game time, score, players in play, and possession of all game balls.

C. Suspended games should be resumed as soon as possible after it has become safe to resume play.

3.6.2.2. Resuming a suspended game:

A. All players in play at the suspension must line up behind their respective starting lines.

   i. If, while play was suspended, a player became too injured to play, had to leave the event, or otherwise became unavailable to play, another player on the roster may substitute in, starting on the line in their place.

B. Game balls must be given to the appropriate teams based on the possession information recorded at the time the game was suspended.

   i. Any balls which were not possessed when play was stopped shall be placed on the ball marks.

      a. The inner marks shall be filled first.

      b. If there were two loose bludgers, but the quaffle was possessed, both inner marks shall be used for the bludgers.

C. If the suspension occurred after the snitch runner was released, then the snitch runner should enter the player area before the game resumes and the seekers must line up behind their starting lines.

   i. Any snitch handicaps that had been implemented

prior to the suspension are still in effect when the game resumes.

D. The head referee shouts "Brooms Down!"

E. All starting players should be stationary with the broom flat on the ground as in the regular start of game procedure.

F. The head referee shouts "Ready!"

G. The head referee shouts "Brooms Up!"

    i. On the first "B" sound of "Brooms Up!" all players may begin play.

4. Scoring

4.1. GOAL SCORING

4.1.1. Good goal

Ten points are scored for a team when the quaffle in any way passes entirely through their opponent's hoops and the goal is confirmed as good. The head referee must confirm that a goal is good.

A. The following must all be true for a goal to be counted as good:
  i. The whole quaffle passes through one of the hoops.
    a. Any part (or the entirety) of the scoring player's body may pass through the hoop.
    b. Goals may be scored through either side of the hoops.
  ii. The scoring player (the player who propels the quaffle before it enters the hoops) is not knocked out while in contact with the quaffle, making it unscorable (See: 5.3.4. Natural motion).
  iii. The scoring player has not committed a back to hoops foul immediately before receiving the quaffle or while in contact with a live quaffle.
  iv. There is no delayed penalty, blue card, yellow card, or red card offense committed by the scoring team in the bludger or quaffle game (See: 3.3.5. Delayed penalties).

      a. Penalties occurring solely between the seekers or between a seeker and a snitch runner do not negate a goal (See: 3.3.5.3.B.v.b.).

    v. The hoop is not dislodged or otherwise unplayable (See: 4.2. Broken or fallen hoops).

B. The quaffle becomes dead as soon as a good goal has been scored. If a goal is confirmed as good, then play should proceed as described in 4.4. Restarting after a goal.

C. The head referee must confirm that a goal is good.

    i. The head referee confirms that the goal is good by blowing one long whistle blast and raising both arms.

    ii. The quaffle should be played as if it is live until the head referee confirms that the goal is good.

      a. If the goal is declared good, then no plays with the quaffle during this time count, though all fouls and illegal plays would still result in a penalty.

      b. If the goal is declared no good, then the quaffle is live and play continues.

4.1.2. Own goal

A team may score a goal for the opposition by passing the quaffle through a goal in their own keeper zone.

A. Any time a live quaffle passes through a hoop, and the above conditions are met, a goal is scored.

B. If an own goal is scored, then the goal counts for the opposition, no matter which team propelled the ball through the hoop.

4.2. BROKEN OR FALLEN HOOPS

4.2.1. Scoring through a dislodged or broken

hoop

No one may score on a hoop that has become dislodged. A dislodged hoop is defined as being broken, displaced, in any way knocked down, or unplayable.

A. If a hoop is in the process of becoming dislodged when the quaffle passes completely through it, the goal still counts.
   i. A falling hoop is considered fully dislodged when the hoop loop touches the ground, or the hoop otherwise comes to at least temporary rest in a non-upright and intact position, including on top of a player.
   ii. A hoop must be entirely fixed and returned to its correct position before a goal may again be scored on that hoop.
   iii. Hoops that are no longer along the same plane as the hoop line (i.e. turned so that they are no longer facing the midfield line) are not considered dislodged and may be scored upon, but they should be returned to the proper position by the corresponding goal judge once active play leaves the area.
   iv. The head referee may verbally declare any hoop dislodged, and therefore unplayable, if the referee determines that the above conditions for a dislodged hoop are met.

4.2.2. Dislodged hoop procedure

A. If a hoop is broken, displaced or otherwise unplayable:
   i. Play must be stopped if the broken hoop poses a threat to the safety of the players.
   ii. If play is not stopped, the goal judge must return the hoop to its proper position as soon as play leaves the

area.

    iii. If the quaffle goes past the hard boundary and there are no advantages, play must be stopped to fix the hoops.

    iv. The team with the quaffle may elect to request play be stopped to fix a dislodged hoop if the quaffle or the player with the quaffle has not passed the midfield line on that possession.

        a. Once the team possesses the quaffle within, or propels the quaffle into their opponent's half of the player area, the team may not request play to be stopped under this rule, even if the team brings the quaffle back into their own half.

            1. The possession is considered over when the opposing team gains possession of the quaffle.

B. If all three of a team's hoops are broken, the head referee must stop play until they are fixed.

C. No players may play in a manner that would create a significant threat of dislodging the hoops.

    i. This rule does not apply in the following instances:

        a. A hoop is dislodged by a thrown ball.

        b. An offensive quaffle player dislodges a hoop while attempting a contested score.

        c. A defensive quaffle player dislodges a hoop as a result of their own physical interaction with an offensive quaffle player who is attempting to score.

D. A player may not intentionally dislodge a hoop.

E. A player may not affect the position of a hoop, including intentionally tilting the pole or spinning the loop, with the intent of affecting whether the quaffle will pass through it.

⚑ *Penalty: Blue*—A player who repeatedly, unintentionally dislodges a hoop must receive a blue card.

🏳 *Penalty: Yellow*—A player who recklessly dislodges a hoop must receive a yellow card.

🏳 *Penalty: Red*—A player who intentionally dislodges a hoop must receive a red card.

🏳 *Penalty: Red*—A player who affects the position of a hoop with the intent of affecting whether the quaffle will pass through it must receive a red card.

4.3. GOALTENDING

A play is considered goaltending, and is scored as if the quaffle had gone through the hoop, if any of the following is true:

A. A player, other than the keeper, touches the quaffle with a part of themselves or their equipment that is extended through a hoop, within their own defensive keeper zone, from the side where the quaffle would exit.

B. A player, other than the keeper, blocks the quaffle from passing entirely through a hoop, within their own defensive keeper zone, by positioning themselves or their equipment on the opposite side of the hoop from where the quaffle would enter the hoop.

🏳 *Penalty: Red*—A beater or seeker who intentionally goaltends must receive a red card.

4.4. RESTARTING AFTER A GOAL

4.4.1. Penalty box release

If there are players in the penalty box when the opposing

team scores a goal, one player from the team scored upon with the least amount of penalty time remaining for a blue or yellow card is released from the penalty box. Players serving stacked time are released after two goals. Players serving time in the penalty box for red card offenses are not released after a goal (See: 9.2.2. Time of penalty).

4.4.2. Dead quaffle

During the time between when a goal is confirmed as good by the head referee and when quaffle play is restarted, all of the players and all of the balls except for the quaffle are live and in play. However, the quaffle is dead, and no one may score with the quaffle until quaffle play is restarted. The following conditions apply to the quaffle while it is dead:

A. Any player on the formerly defending keeper's team may carry or pass the quaffle to the keeper in that keeper's own keeper zone, but may not otherwise interact with the dead quaffle.

    i. Substitutes may pass the dead quaffle to their keeper in this manner, but must always remain in the substitution area or bench while doing so.

B. The formerly offensive team may not pick up or otherwise move the quaffle unless they are providing it to the keeper at the formerly defending team's request.

    i. The formerly offensive team may choose to decline that request.

C. The formerly defending keeper may request that a referee deliver the quaffle, but the referee may only deliver the quaffle in the team's own keeper zone.

D. If a penalty turns over a dead quaffle to the formerly

offensive team, the quaffle becomes live upon the restart after the turnover.

🏴 *Penalty: Blue*—A player who intentionally illegally interacts with a dead quaffle must receive a blue card.

4.4.3. Keeper restart

After a goal has been scored, quaffle play is restarted when the quaffle is in the possession of the formerly defending team's keeper on that keeper's team's own half of the field.

4.4.3.1.—If the formerly defending keeper is the first player to possess the dead quaffle, it becomes live if they possess it anywhere in their half of the field.

A. If anyone else touches the quaffle first, including a referee or opponent (upon the keeper's team's request), then it must be reset in the keeper zone, and the keeper must retreat to their own keeper zone to restart play.

4.4.3.2.—The head referee must blow one short whistle blast after quaffle play is restarted by the keeper's possession.

4.5. THE SNITCH CATCH

4.5.1. The snitch catch

When a snitch catch is confirmed, 30 points are awarded to the team whose seeker caught the snitch, and the period of play is immediately ended. A good snitch catch is confirmed when all of the following are true:

A. A seeker has detached the snitch ball from the snitch runner and holds sole possession of the snitch ball during the instant that it is separated from the snitch runner.

B. The snitch ball was securely attached to the shorts of the snitch runner before the snitch catch.

C. The snitch runner was not on the ground or ruled as down during the snitch catch (See: 8.3.9. Ruled as down).

D. There is no foul of any level (back to hoops to red card) by the seeker who caught the snitch immediately prior to or during the catch.

E. The catch did not occur between a foul by any member of the catching team resulting in a card and the time the card was given to the player.

F. The snitch was not physically impeded by any game official or member of the catching team in a way that may have in any way contributed to the catch, even if unintentional.

G. The seeker was not knocked out or dismounted at the time of the catch.

H. The seekers did not simultaneously remove the snitch from the snitch runner.

I. Play was not stopped when the snitch was caught.

4.5.2. Snitch catch procedure

A. If snitch referee believes that there may have been a good snitch catch, the snitch referee must blow paired short whistle blasts to stop play (See: 8.3.6. Confirming the catch).

   i. All plays made before this stoppage are valid and must be counted except as described in rule 4.5.2.C.i.

B. The head referee, snitch referee, snitch runner, and any other relevant officials should confer to determine if the catch is good.

C. If the catch is confirmed:

i. If the snitch runner or another game official has clear knowledge that the successful snitch catch was made prior to an otherwise good goal, that goal must be disallowed.

ii. The head referee blows three long whistle blasts, 30 points are awarded to the catching team, and the period of play ends immediately.

4.5.3. Declining the catch

In limited situations, when a goal or no-goal call is reversed pursuant to rule 8.1.3.2.A., the catching team may choose to decline the catch.

A. A snitch catch cannot be declined unless the catch occurred between the original goal or no-goal signal by the head referee and the official reversal of that call pursuant to rule 8.1.3.2.A.

i. If the head referee had not yet signaled their call prior to the catch, the catch cannot be declined, regardless of whether other officials had made any signals.

B. A snitch catch cannot be declined unless the change of the goal call affects whether the period would end in a tie.

C. If a catch is declined, play restarts as though the catch had been ruled no good.

5. The Knockout Effect

5.1. THE MOUNTED BROOM

5.1.1. Mounting the broom

All players must be mounted according to the following procedure in order to participate in play:

A. To mount the broom the player must have the broom straddled between their legs, touching some part of their body.
B. The player remains mounted until one of the following occurs:
   i. The broom (or arm that is holding the broom) no longer crosses the plane between the player's legs.
   ii. The player loses contact with the broom.
   iii. The broom lays flat on the ground without the player's hand underneath it.
C. No forms of artificial attachment are allowed; these are considered illegal equipment (See: 2.4.1.D. Brooms).

5.1.2. Dismounting

If a player intentionally or unintentionally dismounts while in play, any plays made by that player while dismounted do not count.

A. Once dismounted, the player is considered out of play until they have followed the knockout procedure and remounted the broom (See: 5.3. Knockout procedure).

B. If a player is dismounted by the illegal actions of an opponent, the player must immediately remount and continue play. If the player does not immediately remount, then they must follow the procedures for the knockout procedure (See: 6.1.1.1.A. and 5.3. Knockout procedure).

🏳 *Penalty: Back to hoops*—A player who dismounts while in play must be sent back to hoops.

🏳 *Penalty: Blue*—Any player who continues play after being dismounted and affects play must receive a blue card.

🏳 *Penalty: Yellow*—A player who continues or initiates contact while dismounted must receive a yellow card.

5.2. KNOCKOUTS

5.2.1. Incurring the knockout effect

If a player is struck with a live bludger, that player is "knocked out" and must follow the knockout procedure as outlined in 5.3. Knockout procedure.

A. A player is knocked out if that player is struck by a live bludger in the following places:
  i. Any part of the player's body, including the player's hair or fingers, including fingers holding a ball.
  ii. On any part of the player's equipment (including the broom), except for a held ball.
  iii. On any part of the player's clothing.
B. If a live bludger hits a player at the same time as the bludger hits the ground or is caught by another eligible player, the player is still knocked out.

C. If a player is struck by a live bludger, that player is considered "knocked out" unless they are called "safe" or "clear" by a referee.

5.2.2. Live bludger

In order to incur the knockout effect, a bludger must be live.

A. To be live, a bludger:
   i. Must be thrown, kicked, or otherwise intentionally propelled by a beater.
   ii. Must not have touched the ground, traveled outside of the player area, or been caught.
      a. In these cases, the bludger is live until the action indicated has occurred.
   iii. Must not have been stripped by an opponent's body, another bludger, or the quaffle.
B. Any bludger that is not live is considered "dead."
C. Every opposing player struck by a live bludger is subject to the knockout effect.
   i. Chasers, and seekers, and non-protected keepers are immediately knocked out and must complete the knockout procedure (See: 5.3. Knockout procedure).
   ii. Keepers are knocked out immediately, unless they are a protected keeper (See: 7.3.3.2. Keeper-specific powers).
   iii. Beaters who are struck by a live bludger:
      a. May delay dismounting in order to attempt to catch the bludger, until it becomes dead by other means (See: 5.2.4. Struck beater).
         1. If the beater catches the bludger before it becomes dead by other means, they are not knocked out.
         2. If the beater fails to catch the bludger, they are

knocked out.

b. A beater who has been struck by a live bludger may not take any action other than attempting to catch the live bludger that struck them.

5.2.3. Held bludgers

A. A held bludger is not live and does not incur the knockout effect.

B. A beater may not intentionally initiate contact with an opposing player using a held bludger.

   i. A beater may contact another beater with a held bludger in the course of play, but may not hold the bludger against an opposing player to deceive them into believing they are knocked out.

C. A bludger that has been released or propelled in any way, other than by a struck beater, is no longer held and is a live bludger.

⚑ *Penalty: Blue*—A beater who intentionally holds a bludger against an opponent, to make them believe they are knocked out, must receive a blue card.

5.2.4. Struck beater

A struck beater is a beater who has been hit by a live bludger propelled by an opponent.

5.2.4.1. After the initial hit and before the bludger becomes dead, the struck beater may remain on their broom and attempt to catch the live bludger that struck them.

A. The only actions a struck beater may initiate are:

   i. Dropping a held bludger.

    ii. Following the knockout procedure.

    iii. Attempting to catch the live bludger that struck them.

        a. After the initial hit, a beater may not intentionally attempt to change the direction of a bludger in any manner other than to attempt to catch it.

        b. A beater is allowed to propel a bludger further into the air in the process of attempting a catch.

B. If a struck beater takes any actions other than those outlined in 5.2.4.1.A., they are subject to the same rules and penalties for those actions as a knocked out player.

C. If the beater catches the bludger before it otherwise becomes dead, that beater is no longer subject to the knockout effect and the bludger becomes dead.

    i. If the beater is struck by additional live bludgers propelled by opponents after they have become a struck beater, the beater must also catch those bludgers before they otherwise become dead in order to no longer be subject to the knockout effect.

D. If the beater fails to catch the bludger before it becomes dead, the beater must immediately begin the knockout procedure.

⚑ *Penalty: Blue*—A beater who intentionally changes, or makes an attempt to intentionally change, the direction of a bludger after the initial hit must receive a blue card, except where the attempt is on the live bludger which stuck them as part of an attempt to catch it.

5.2.5. Blocking bludgers

A player in possession of a ball may attempt to block an incoming live bludger with the ball in their possession:

A. A quaffle or bludger may be used in an attempt to block.
B. To be a successful block, the incoming bludger must not hit any part of the player, before or after hitting the ball being used to block. This includes, but is not limited to:
   i. The hand holding the ball being used in the attempt to block the bludger.
   ii. Any part of the player's body, including the player's hair or fingers.
   iii. Any part of the player's equipment (including the broom).
   iv. Any part of the player's clothing.
C. The ball used in an attempt to block may be used to bat, swat, or otherwise propel the incoming bludger away from the intended target.
   i. The quaffle, whether it is held or thrown, may not be used to intentionally interact with a bludger which the player was reasonably aware to be either dead or made live by a teammate, including a bludger that is still in the hand of a beater.

5.2.6. Swatting bludgers

Any attempt to bat away, swat, or otherwise intentionally propel a live bludger during an initial hit to a player is considered a bludger swat.

A. Beaters may make any attempt to alter the course of a live bludger provided:
   i. The swat does not cause the bludger to exit the pitch.
   ii. The beater is not already a struck beater (See: 5.2.4.

Struck beater).

B. Chasers and keepers may not swat bludgers at any time unless they are doing so with a quaffle in the process of a block as noted in 5.2.5.C.

C. Seekers may not swat bludgers at any time.

🏳 *Penalty: Blue*—A chaser, seeker, or keeper who illegally swats a bludger at any time must receive a blue card.

5.2.7. Safe Calls

No player can be knocked out by a dead bludger or while immune from the knockout effect. If a player is struck by a bludger which cannot knock them out, the referee shall call that player "safe" or "clear" unless another bludger knocks out the player.

5.2.7.1. Friendly fire

When a bludger is made live by one team, no player on that team may be knocked out by that bludger until it becomes dead and is made live again by the opposing team. Players stuck by friendly fire shall be called "safe" or "clear" unless another bludger knocks out the player.

5.2.7.2. Safe call procedure

A. Players struck by a bludger should dismount and begin the knockout procedure immediately (unless the player is a beater attempting to catch the live bludger).

i. Players must be called "safe" or "clear" by a referee if they are not knocked out by the bludger.

ii. If a player is not called "safe" or "clear" by a referee, then that player is subject to the knockout effect.

B. If the player dismounts due to being stuck by a bludger but is called "safe" or "clear" on that bludger hit and has not made any plays or other actions while dismounted, the referee may allow the player to remount and continue play.

   i. If the referee does not explicitly inform the player to remount and resume play, the player must complete the knockout procedure.

C. If the player fails to begin the knockout procedure immediately:

   i. And the final call on that bludger hit is "safe" or "clear" play shall continue and no penalty shall apply.

   ii. And a referee called the player "safe" or "clear" but the call changes to "beat," the player shall receive no penalty for failing to dismount, as long as the player responds to the "beat" call by dismounting.

   iii. If no referee called the player "safe" or "clear" and the final call on that bludger hit is "beat," the player shall be considered to be willfully ignoring being knocked out.

   a. If the referee believes that the player was unaware that the bludger touched them, then the referee may treat it as an unnoticed knockout.

      1. A player's belief that they are otherwise safe from the bludger shall not be taken into consideration when determining any appropriate penalty.

5.2.8. Knockout immunity

In certain situations, beaters may become immune to the knockout effect by following certain procedures.

5.2.8.1. When a team has possession of two bludgers and the opposing team does not have possession of a bludger:

A. A beater on the team with no bludgers may raise a hand above their shoulder, fist closed, to gain immunity from the knockout effect and attempt to retrieve the free bludger. The following guidelines apply:

    i. The free bludger must become dead before a beater may begin to raise a fist to signal for immunity.

    ii. If an opponent begins a natural motion on an attempted knockout before an immune beater has gained possession of a ball, the knockout does not count (See: 5.3.4. Natural motion).

    iii. If the opponent has released the bludger before a beater claiming immunity has raised a fist above their shoulder, the knockout still counts.

    iv. The player must directly and immediately proceed to gain possession of the free bludger.

        a. This does not prohibit a player from approaching the ball from any direction they prefer.

    v. The player may take no other actions until the free bludger is recovered or otherwise moved.

    vi. If the opposing team loses possession of one of the two bludgers they had possessed, or moves the free bludger in a legal manner, then the beater with immunity immediately loses immunity and must lower their hand.

B. If both beaters on a team raise their fists for immunity, either beater can put their fist back down without penalty. If both beaters keep their fists up, a penalty may be issued.

📛 *Penalty: Back to hoops*—If both beaters on a team raise their fists for immunity and one does not put their fist back down, the referee may send the beater whose call was more likely to be deceptive back to hoops.

🏴 *Penalty: Back to hoops*—A player who unintentionally illegally claims immunity may be sent back to hoops, in place of receiving a blue card, at the discretion of the referee based on whether or not the illegal claim affected gameplay.

🏴 *Penalty: Blue*—A player who affects gameplay with an illegal immunity claim, or who knowingly illegally claims immunity must receive a blue card.

🏴 *Penalty: Blue*—A player who raises a hand with a closed fist and takes any action, other than attempting to recover the free bludger, must receive a blue card.

5.2.8.2. Manipulating immunity—It is illegal to manipulate the status of the bludgers for the sole purpose of changing the state of immunity.

- A. Examples of manipulating immunity include:
    - i. A player claiming immunity after that player has released a bludger, unless the bludger was released in an attempt to incur the knockout effect.
    - ii. A player claiming immunity in an attempt to retrieve a free bludger before that bludger is dead.
    - iii. A player on the team with two bludgers releases a bludger without attempting to knock out an opposing player except when relinquishing the bludger to their opponent or the opponent's hoops.
        - a. An opposing beater who has claimed immunity maintains their immunity when this foul is committed.
- B. If a player manipulates the immunity status of another

player, the referee must inform the other players that the immunity status has not changed.

🚩 *Penalty: Back to hoops*—A player who, at the discretion of the referee, tries to manipulate the status of immunity, must be sent back to hoops.

5.3. KNOCKOUT PROCEDURE

5.3.1. Knockout procedure

After being struck by a bludger resulting in the knockout effect, a player must complete the following procedure, in order, before becoming eligible to participate in the game:

A. Immediately give up possession of any ball by dropping it.
   i. The player must not pass, toss, roll, or kick the ball, unless completing a natural motion already begun (See: 5.3.4. Natural motion).
   ii. A bludger dropped in this way is dead.
   iii. A quaffle dropped in this way is unscorable.
B. Dismount from their broom.
C. Retreat back to their own hoops and touch part of any hoop.
   i. The player must touch the hoop loop or pole, not the hoop base.
   ii. The player must touch the hoop with some part of the player's body, not with the broom.
D. Remount their broom immediately, before leaving the vicinity of the hoops.

🚩 *Penalty: Repeat*—A player who fails to dismount or remounts their broom before touching the hoops during the knockout procedure must repeat the procedure properly.

🏴 *Penalty: Blue*—A knocked out player who interacts with play, other than initiating physical contact (See: 5.3.2.D.i.), without having completed the knockout procedure must receive a blue card.

🏴 *Penalty: Yellow*—A player who intentionally or repeatedly does not complete any part of the knockout procedure must receive a yellow card.

5.3.2. Knocked out players

Knocked out players are out of play and are subject to the following restrictions. A knocked out player must:

A. Not make any play. Any goal, snitch catch, or knockout attempted by a player while they are knocked out is not counted.

B. Not release a pass, shot, or any other action regarding a game ball other than in cases of natural motion (See: 5.3.4. Natural motion).

C. Drop any balls that are currently possessed.

D. Avoid interactions with other players or initiating physical contact.

   i. A player may not initiate any physical contact, other than incidental contact, after having been hit by a live bludger.

   ii. If a player has already initiated physical contact, they should cease contact upon being hit with a live bludger.

   iii. If a player is in the final motion of a singular action or has begun a physical interaction before being hit by a live bludger, then they may complete that action.

   a. If a beater is in the process of wrapping an opposing

       beater, then they may complete the wrap, but may not complete a tackle.

    b. If a chaser is charging an opposing chaser and is hit within the last step, then they should not be penalized for the charge.

    c. If a chaser is charging an opposing chaser and is hit several steps before delivering the charge and still does so, then they should be penalized.

E. Not substitute out of the game.

F. Notice and comply with the referee's call that the player is knocked out.

🏴 *Penalty: Turnover*—A player releasing a pass, shot, or beat attempt after having been knocked out, except in cases of natural motion, results in a turnover to the opposing team.

🏴 *Penalty: Yellow*—Any player who initiates physical contact, other than incidental contact or in the final singular natural motion, with an opposing player while knocked out or as a struck beater must receive a yellow card.

5.3.3. Unnoticed knockout

If a player unintentionally continues play after being hit by a live bludger:

A. The referee should verbally and visually inform the player that the player has been knocked out.

B. The referee may stop play in order to inform the player that they have been knocked out. If the referee must stop play due to an unnoticed knockout:

    i. Any ball held by the player should be turned over to

the closest eligible player of the opposing team.

ii. Any ball illegally propelled by the player after being struck by the live bludger should be turned over to the eligible player of the opposing team closest to the location of the ball when it was illegally propelled.

iii. The player should be sent back to hoops.

C. If a player continues play after failing to realize that they were hit by a live bludger, and affects play, they are subject to additional penalty, despite their lack of knowledge of the knockout.

🏴 *Penalty: Blue*—A player who unintentionally continues play after being hit by a live bludger and affects play, other than in cases of throwing a ball (See: 5.3.4. Natural motion) or initiating physical contact (See: 5.3.2. Knocked out players), must receive a blue card.

🏴 *Penalty: Yellow*—A player who willfully ignores being knocked out must receive a yellow card.

5.3.4. Natural motion

When a player is knocked out, that player may finish one singular natural motion that they had already started, if that motion cannot be reasonably stopped.

5.3.4.1. For natural motion to be called on a pass, beat, or shot, the following conditions apply:

A. The player must release any possessed ball as part of the singular natural motion begun before being struck by a live bludger.

i. Any motion begun after the bludger struck the player

does not qualify as a natural motion.

B. If a player has begun the final, singular movement of a pass when knocked out, the player may release the ball and play continues normally.

    i. A player may not release the ball if they are struck by a live bludger during any additional motions before the final motion, including, but not limited to, a windup.

C. A player who has not yet contacted a ball when they become knocked out is not allowed to move that ball, even if they contact it in one singular natural motion.

    i. If a ball bounces off a knocked out player in a way that they could not reasonably avoid, and that player does not propel that ball, no penalty shall apply.

D. If a player is no longer touching the quaffle when they are struck by a live bludger, the quaffle does not become unscorable.

E. A beater who is in the process of releasing a bludger may finish the natural motion, but this bludger is dead and cannot incur a knockout until it is made live another way.

F. If the release of a ball is ruled to be simultaneous with the player being struck by a live bludger, the released ball shall be considered an unscorable quaffle or dead bludger.

🏴 *Penalty: Turnover*—If a player unintentionally begins a new motion or otherwise unintentionally propels a ball after being knocked out, the ball they moved must be turned over to the opposing team.

🏴 *Penalty: Yellow*—Any player who intentionally begins an illegal action, with knowledge that they were knocked out (including, but not limited to, being informed by a referee), should receive a yellow card.

5.3.4.2. Unscorable quaffle—If a player is touching the quaffle when struck by a live bludger propelled by an opponent and releases it or otherwise propels it according to natural motion, the quaffle becomes an unscorable quaffle.

- A. An unscorable quaffle cannot result in a goal, even if the quaffle goes entirely through a hoop.
- B. A referee must send the knocked out player back to hoops and call any goal no good.
- C. The quaffle remains live and play continues normally.
- D. An unscorable quaffle that bounces off a player from the opposing team, a referee, any equipment, or the ground remains unscorable.
- E. The quaffle becomes scorable again if:
    - i. It is touched by a quaffle player teammate of the player who released the unscorable quaffle.
    - ii. It is possessed by any player.

6. Player Conduct and Interactions

6.1. GENERAL PLAYER CONDUCT

6.1.1. Rules and regulations

6.1.1.1. Authority of rules—Players shall abide by all rules and regulations in force for a particular game or tournament.

    A. Any player who is in violation of a rule as a direct result of the illegal actions of an opponent must immediately correct the violation once the opponent's action is completed in order to avoid penalty.

⚑ *Penalty: General*—Any player who violates a rule or regulation in force for a specific game or tournament shall be subject to the appropriate penalty as established in this rulebook.

6.1.1.2. Authority of referees—Players must abide by the directives of the referees assigned to a particular game.

⚑ *Penalty: Yellow*—A player who refuses to comply with a referee's directive must receive a yellow card.

6.1.2. Unsporting behavior

Players must abide by standards of sporting behavior in all interactions with players, spectators, officials, and event staff.

6.1.2.1. Players must not taunt or engage in rude or antagonistic behavior with players, spectators, officials, and event staff.

🏳 *Penalty: Yellow*—A player who taunts opponents or engages in rude or antagonistic behavior toward players, spectators, officials, or event staff must receive a yellow card.

🏳 *Penalty: Red*—A player who directs explicit or threatening taunts toward opponents or engages in explicitly rude or hostile behavior toward players, spectators, officials, or event staff must receive a red card.

6.1.2.2. Language and gestures—It is illegal to use explicit, vulgar, extreme, or abusive language or gestures at any time.

🏳 *Penalty: Warning*—A player who uses undirected explicit, vulgar, extreme, or abusive language or gestures must receive a warning.

🏳 *Penalty: Blue*—A player who uses undirected explicit language or gestures after being warned may receive a blue card.

🏳 *Penalty: Yellow*—A player who uses explicit language or gestures directed toward any person must receive a yellow card.

🏳 *Penalty: Red*—A player who uses extreme or abusive language or obscene gestures directed toward any person must receive a red card.

6.1.2.3. Physical altercations and threats—It is illegal to engage in physical altercations with or threaten any players, spectators, officials, or event staff.

🏳 *Penalty: Red*—A player who engages in physical altercations with or threatens any players, spectators, officials, or event staff must receive a red card

6.1.2.4. Serious foul play—It is illegal to commit serious foul play, including egregious conduct and flagrant cheating.

🚩 *Penalty: Red*—A player who commits serious foul play must receive a red card.

🚩 *Penalty: Special*—If a team commits foul play that cannot be attributed to a specific player, the speaking captain must receive a red card.

6.1.2.5. Faking a foul—It is illegal to pretend to be fouled in an attempt to deceive a referee.

🚩 *Penalty: Yellow*—A player who pretends to be fouled must receive a yellow card.

6.2. SUBSTITUTIONS

6.2.1. Substitution guidelines

A. Jurisdiction over substitutes—All substitutes and team staff (such as coaches) are subject to the authority and jurisdiction of the referees.
B. Time of substitution—A substitution may be made at any time during the game, provided a referee has not stopped play.
C. All substitutions must result in the substituting team adhering to all rules governing the number of players allowed at each position and the gender maximum rule (See: 7.1.1. Rosters and players and 7.1.3. Gender maximum rule).
D. No player may substitute or change positions while in the

penalty box, with the following exceptions:

i. A keeper sent to the penalty box must change positions with a chaser before entering the box.

ii. A player who has been given a red card must immediately leave the player area and a substitute must proceed to the penalty box, following the red card procedure (See: 9.1.5. Red card).

iii. When a substitute commits a foul, the team captain must choose a player to remove from the pitch while the substitute is in the penalty box and the substitute must serve the penalty time as the position of that player.

iv. A speaking captain who is on the player roster is sent to the penalty box for a team penalty:

    a. If in play—The speaking captain may not change positions, unless they are the keeper, and must report immediately to the penalty box to serve the penalty time.

    b. If not in play—The speaking captain must designate a player to leave the pitch and must serve the penalty time as the position of the fouling player.

        1. If the penalty is a red card, the player pulled off the pitch must serve the penalty time, and the speaking captain must leave the player area.

v. If the head referee deems a fouling player too injured to continue play by serving in the penalty box:

    a. The speaking captain must choose an eligible substitute.

    b. The fouling player may not reenter play until after the substitute has been released from the penalty box.

    c. The scorekeeper and head referee should ensure that the fouling player is the one who has been credited with the foul.

    vi. An injured player is the only player on the pitch at their position, and there are no eligible substitutes:

        a. The speaking captain must designate a player on the pitch, who is not the last player at their own position, to switch to the injured player's position and move to the injured player's location.

6.2.2. Substitution procedure

To replace a player with a substitute, the following conditions must be observed:

A. The player substituting out is not knocked out or dismounted.

B. The player substituting out must not carry any balls off the pitch.

C. The player substituting out exits the pitch boundary within the team's substitute area and dismounts.

    i. The player must not dismount before crossing the pitch boundary.

    ii. The player substituting out is no longer eligible to be knocked out once the player has dismounted.

D. The substitute entering play must mount the broom and step onto the pitch before interacting with play, even if play is occurring off the pitch.

E. If any other equipment must be traded (including headbands) this must occur off the pitch.

F. The substitute enters the pitch along the boundary of the team's substitute area.

G. A substitution is complete when the substitute crosses the boundary of the team's substitute area back onto the pitch.

H. The substitute is then immediately eligible to engage in gameplay and is eligible to be knocked out.

6.2.2.1. Unlimited substitution—By following the procedure in 6.2.2. Substitution procedure, a player who has substituted out may replace another player, of any position, at any time later in the game.

🏴 *Penalty: Repeat*—If a team attempting a substitution violates part of the substitution procedure, the referee must clearly alert the players and they must repeat the full substitution procedure. If the player exiting the pitch was dismounted or had been knocked out, that player must complete the knockout procedure before completing the substitution procedure (See: 5.3. Knockout procedure).

🏴 *Penalty: Blue*—If a player who has entered the pitch as a result of an illegal substitution disregards the referee's command to repeat the substitution or interacts with a ball or opponent, then they must receive a blue card.

6.2.3. Position change

A. Players may change positions by exchanging headbands or by both players switching to the proper headband color for their new position.
B. If two players who are in play change positions, they must follow the full procedure for substitutions with the following exception:
   i. A keeper being sent to the penalty box must immediately exchange headbands with a chaser. This may be done on the pitch (See: 6.4.2.6.B. Unusual penalty box situations).

🏴 *Penalty: Repeat*—If players complete an illegal position change, they may switch back to their original positions and complete the change properly as long as neither has interacted with play in any way during the time before the foul is corrected.

🏴 *Penalty: Double blue*—If either player interacts with play after an illegal position change, both players must receive blue cards.

6.2.4. Substitutions due to injury

A. If a player is injured and play is not stopped, the substitution must follow all of the substitution procedure as outlined in 6.2.2. Substitution procedure.

B. A player may not feign an injury for any reason.

C. If a player is injured and play is stopped:
   i. Game time, seeker floor time, and penalty time must all be stopped.
   ii. The injured player's broom is dropped on the field where the player was located.
   iii. The injured player leaves the pitch.
      a. If play is stopped for an injury, the player must leave the pitch and must follow the substitution procedure to return to the pitch.
      b. The player may be assisted in leaving the pitch by any necessary means.
   iv. The injured player must be replaced by an eligible substitute.
      a. While play is stopped, the substitute puts on all necessary equipment and goes to the point on the pitch indicated by the injured player's broom, replacing the player.
      b. If there is no eligible substitute for an injured player,

a team may continue playing a player down.

1. If this injured player is the only player at their position, the speaking captain must designate a player on the pitch, who is not the last player at their own position, to switch to the injured player's position and move to the injured player's location

⚑ *Penalty: Yellow*—A player who feigns an injury must receive a yellow card.

6.2.5. Substitute area

Substitutes must remain within the substitute area, as defined in 2.1.5.1., when play is not stopped. The following exceptions apply:

A. When not about to enter play, all players must remain within their team bench, as defined in 2.1.5.2. Team benches.

B. The team's speaking captain, who has been designated before the game, or that person's replacement, may leave this area to communicate with referees, tournament staff, or players on the team.

C. Any players in need of medical attention may leave the substitute area to receive medical attention.

    i. If necessary, anyone designated by the team's speaking captain may leave the substitute area to attend to an injured player.

    ii. All players who leave the substitute area in this way remain eligible to return to the game, if they are medically cleared.

D. Any player who receives a red card must leave the player

area and follow all tournament specific provisions (See: 9.1.5. Red card).

🏴 *Penalty: Blue*—A substitute who intentionally and illegally leaves the substitute area or bench without permission of the referee may receive a blue card if their actions directly affected gameplay.

🏴 *Penalty: Blue*—A substitute who intentionally and illegally leaves the substitute area or bench with the intent of circumventing other rules must be given a blue card.

6.2.6. Substitutes interfering with play

A substitute may not interfere with play in any way. The following guidelines apply:

A. A substitute may not intentionally interact with a player or ball during play, including any play that occurs outside of the pitch boundaries.
B. If play moves towards a substitute, that substitute must make every reasonable effort to get out of the way.

🏴 *Penalty: Blue*—A substitute who does not make every reasonable effort to move out of the way of play must receive a blue card.

🏴 *Penalty: Red*—A substitute who intentionally interacts with play must receive a red card.

6.2.7. Substitutions between periods

Teams may make any number of substitutions during the time between periods without following substitution procedure. Once a period has begun, however, all procedures must be followed.

A. Any player serving time in the penalty box may not be substituted out between periods.

B. If any player receives a penalty card for a foul occurring after the head referee signaled the end of the period, it shall be treated as a penalty against a substitute, and the speaking captain may choose the position at which the penalty shall be served.

🚩 *Penalty: Red*—Any player who intentionally breaks the substitution rules in order to affect gameplay is guilty of serious foul play and must receive a red card.

6.3. PHYSICAL INTERACTIONS

6.3.1. General interactions

6.3.1.1. Legal contact—Players are allowed to physically interact over the course of play.

A. Bumping, grappling, and incidental contact between players of the same position, and chasers and keepers in regard to one another, is legal in most circumstances.

B. Other particular forms of contact are legal in some circumstances and illegal in others (See: 6.3.2. Specific contact).

C. Illegal contact—Illegal contact includes any form of contact prohibited by the rules. Illegal contact may be intentional or unintentional. In some cases, unintentional illegal physical contact may be adjusted to avoid penalty. In order to be considered unintentional, the offending player must act immediately to correct the illegal contact.

6.3.1.2. Illegal physical contact—The following forms of physical contact are always illegal, unless the contact is determined by the referee to have been incidental:

A. Intentionally contacting a player of another position, except for chasers and keepers in regard to one another.

B. Intentionally contacting the snitch runner, except for seekers.

C. Kicking an opponent.

D. Kneeing an opponent.

E. Head-butting an opponent.

F. Making forcible contact using the crown of the head.

G. Elbowing an opponent.

H. Making contact with an opponent's head, neck, or groin.

I. Initiating contact at or below the knees of an opponent.

J. Exerting force at or below the knees of an opponent.

K. Tripping an opponent.

L. Sliding or diving into an opponent.

M. Jumping or leaping onto any player.

N. Attaching a body to another player so that the player who initiates the contact is being carried by the opposing player.

O. Intentionally lifting or continuing to hold another player off the ground, either an opponent or player from the same team.

P. Contacting an opposing protected keeper who is in sole possession of the quaffle (See: 7.3.3.2. Keeper-specific powers).

🏴 *Penalty: Back to hoops*—A player who unintentionally makes illegal physical contact and immediately adjusts to correct the contact may be sent back to hoops at the discretion of the referee based on whether or not the physical contact affected gameplay.

📫 *Penalty: Yellow*—A player who makes illegal physical contact either intentionally, without immediately adjusting, or in a way that affects gameplay must receive a yellow card.

📫 *Penalty: Red*—A player who makes illegal physical contact in a way that the referee determines to be violent or egregious conduct must receive a red card.

6.3.1.3. Picks—A pick is when a player gets to a legal position on the field in the path of an opposing player for the purpose of slowing down the opposing player or making them change direction without initially engaging in a push, charge, or wrap.

- A. A pick is considered set once the picking player positions themselves in the anticipated path of their opponent.
- B. It is illegal to pick a player of another position, except for keepers and chasers with regard to each other.
- C. It is illegal to pick a player in such a way that it causes an opponent to run into a single point of the picking player's body (such as an elbow or the point of the shoulder).
- D. If the player initiates contact with an extended or extending arm, this shall be considered a push rather than a pick or other form of contact.
  - i. This does not apply if the player makes contact using their torso before the arm is extended. If this is the case, the contact will be considered a push in addition to the contact's original designation.
- E. The player's feet do not need to be set in order for the play to be legal.
  - i. If the would-be picking player is moving directly at their opponent during the pick, and contact is forceful, the play will instead be considered a charge.

F. If neither player has possession of a ball, the following additional restrictions apply:

   i. A pick set from behind must initially give that player a step of room to stop and/or change direction.

   ii. A pick set on a moving player must be set with enough time for the player to stop and/or change direction, as determined by the picked player's speed at the time that the pick is set, not by their actual awareness of the pick.

      a. The picked player must make every attempt to avoid charging the picking player, either by slowing down so that the initiation of contact is non-forceful, or by avoiding the opposing player entirely.

         1. Incidental contact shall not be penalized.

      b. If the picked player charges the picking player and the pick was set in violation of 6.3.1.3.F.ii., they shall not receive a penalty for charging a player without possession unless they attempt to add force to the charge in reaction to the pick.

G. If the picked player reacts to the pick by changing their path, any motion to move into the new path shall be considered a new pick.

🚩 *Penalty: Back to hoops*—A player who sets an unintentionally illegal pick and immediately adjusts to correct the interaction may be sent back to hoops at the discretion of the referee based on whether or not the physical interaction affected gameplay.

🚩 *Penalty: Yellow*—A player who sets an illegal pick that is either intentional, not immediately adjusted, or in a way that affects gameplay must receive a yellow card.

🚩 *Penalty: General*—A player who illegally charges a player who is picking them is subject to the penalties for an illegal charge (See: 6.3.2.5.).

6.3.1.4. Kicking a contested ball—It is generally legal to kick a ball which an opponent is attempting to play. The following rules apply:

A. A player must not kick any opponent.
   i. If the referee determines that the kicked player was at fault for being kicked because they moved into the way of the kick late, no penalty shall apply.
B. If the referee determines that a player's kick did not make contact with the opponent only because the opponent reacted to the kick by actively getting out of the way, the player must be deemed to be playing recklessly.
   i. This rule only applies if the referee determines that the kick would have made contact without the opponent actively getting out of its way.
   ii. No penalty shall apply if the would be kicked player would have been deemed at fault for being kicked under 6.3.1.4.A.i. had contact been made on the kick.
C. If a player narrowly misses an opponent while attempting to kick a ball, and the referee determines that the player was not in control of where the kick went, the player must be deemed to be playing recklessly.

🏳 *Penalty: Yellow*—A player who the referee deems to be playing recklessly must receive a yellow card.

🏳 *Penalty: Yellow*—A player who kicks an opponent while attempting to kick a ball must receive a yellow card.

🏳 *Penalty: Red*—A player who kicks an opponent in a manner

that the referee determines to be violent or egregious conduct must receive a red card.

6.3.1.5. Egregious contact—Particularly egregious illegal contact is prohibited, and the following guidelines apply. A player may not:

A. Make contact using excessive force.
  i. Using excessive force is defined as when a player both exceeds by far the necessary use of force to complete the action initiated and as a result is in danger of injuring an opponent.
B. Deliberately injure or attempt to deliberately injure any person.
C. Strike or attempt to strike an opponent.
D. Intentionally physically contact an opponent's head, neck, or groin.
E. Intentionally physically contact a referee other than the snitch runner.
F. Charge a helpless receiver (See: 6.3.1.10. Helpless receiver).
G. Tackle a helpless receiver (See: 6.3.1.10. Helpless receiver).
H. Intentionally spit at or on a player, spectator, official, or event staff.
I. As a substitute, intentionally contact any person who is in play (See: 6.2.6. Substitutes interfering with play).

🏴 *Penalty: Red*—A player using egregiously illegal physical contact must receive a red card.

6.3.1.6. Initial point of contact—There are several types of physical contact, including pushing, body blocking, charging, grabbing, wrapping, and tackling in which a player must not make initial contact with an opponent from behind.

   A. The contact must be initiated from the front of the opponent's torso:
- i. The front of the torso is defined by a 180 degree straight plane bisecting the player at the middle of both shoulders.
- ii. To be considered to the front of the opponent and to be eligible to make contact, the navel of the player initiating contact must be in front of this 180 degree plane when contact is initiated.
- iii. As long as the body of the contacting player is positioned in this manner the actual point of contact may occur at any legal part of the opponent's torso, arms, or legs above the knee.

   B. Once contact has been legally established, a player may continue contact even when it results in contact from behind.

   C. If the referee determines that a player initiates contact by leading with their back, the opposing player may continue the contact and there is no foul.

   D. If the referee determines that a player spins or turns just prior to contact, causing the opposing player to initiate contact to be from behind, the play may continue and there is no foul for contact from behind.
- i. If the referee determines that the contacting player had enough time to react and avoid contact after the spin, the contact is not exempt from the contact from behind rules.

   E. If a player outruns an opponent attempting to initiate contact and the contact is initiated from behind, this is still a foul. This could be when two players are running for the same ball, or when a defender is facing an offensive player, is passed, and initiates contact from behind after they are passed.

🏴 *Penalty: Back to hoops*—A player who unintentionally makes initial contact from outside the 180 degree plane and immediately adjusts to correct the contact may be sent back to hoops at the discretion of the referee based on whether or not the physical contact affected gameplay.

🏴 *Penalty: Yellow*—A player who makes initial contact from outside of the 180 degree plane, either intentionally, without immediately adjusting, or in a way that affects gameplay, while performing a push, body block, charge, grab, wrap, or tackle must receive a yellow card.

🏴 *Penalty: Red*—A player who makes initial contact from outside of the 180 degree plane in a way that the referee determines to be violent or egregious conduct must receive a red card.

6.3.1.7. Limited contact from behind:

A. For types of contact not listed in 6.3.1.6., a player may make minimal contact from behind, so long as the player does not break any other rules.

B. Limited contact from behind is also allowed in the following circumstances:
    i. While grappling, or jostling for position.
    ii. During an attempt to steal.

C. Even if the contact from behind was initiated legally, in order to then complete any of the physical interactions listed in 6.3.1.6., contact must be discontinued and reinitiated from the front.

6.3.1.8. Adjusting illegal contact:

A. A player who is forced to make illegal contact on an opposing player due to the direct actions of the opposing player must act immediately to readjust the contact to a legal position or discontinue the contact.
  i. If the player has enough time to adjust to a legal position prior to initiating contact, they must do so.
B. A player who initiates contact legally but is forced to continue contact below the knees due to the direct actions of an opponent must discontinue the contact.

🏴 *Penalty: Yellow*—A player who does not readjust or discontinue contact after being forced into an illegal position by an opponent must receive a yellow card.

6.3.1.9. Sliding and diving—Players may slide or dive during the game. However, it is illegal to:

A. Slide or dive into an opponent.
B. Slide or dive directly toward an opponent in a way that forces the opponent to change their movement to get out of the way of the slide or dive.

🏴 *Penalty: Back to hoops*—A player who unintentionally commits an illegal slide or dive and immediately adjusts to correct the interaction may be sent back to hoops at the discretion of the referee based on whether or not the physical interaction affected gameplay.

🏴 *Penalty: Yellow*—A player who commits an illegal slide or dive that is either intentional, not immediately adjusted, or in a way that affects gameplay must receive a yellow card.

🏴 *Penalty: Red*—A player who commits an illegal slide or dive in a manner that the referee determines to be violent or egregious conduct must receive a red card.

6.3.1.10. Helpless receiver—A receiver who is in the process of catching a ball that is in the air is considered a helpless receiver.

  A. A receiver does not have to leave the ground in order to be considered a helpless receiver.
  B. A receiver remains helpless until they establish their footing on the ground after either the receiver has gained sole and complete possession of the ball or they are otherwise no longer attempting to catch the ball.
  C. A helpless receiver may not be pushed, wrapped, charged, or tackled by any opponent.
  D. A player who the referee determines to have thrown a ball to themselves in an attempt to draw a card for illegal contact with a helpless receiver shall not be considered a helpless receiver on that throw.

🏴 *Penalty: General*—A player who initiates a wrap or push on a helpless receiver is subject to the penalties for illegal wraps and pushes respectively (See: 6.3.2.7. Wrapping and 6.3.2.4. Pushing).

🏴 *Penalty: Red*—A player who charges or tackles a helpless receiver must receive a red card.

6.3.2. Specific contact

6.3.2.1. Grappling—Also referred to as touching, this contact consists of placing a hand or hands on an opponent.

A. When to grapple: A player may grapple with any opponent of the same position, and keepers and chasers in regard to one another, at any point during the game.
   i. One or two arms may be used while grappling.
   ii. While grappling, a player may make initial contact with the opposing player outside of the area described under 6.3.1.6.A. This contact does not entitle the player to make other contact with the opponent without releasing and reestablishing contact in accordance with 6.3.1.6.A.
B. Illegal grappling:
   i. A player must not grapple with an opponent at the head, neck, or groin.
   ii. A player must not grapple with an opponent at or below the knees.

⚑ *Penalty: Back to hoops*—A player who commits unintentional illegal grappling and immediately adjusts to correct the contact may be sent back to hoops at the discretion of the referee based on whether or not the physical contact affected gameplay.

⚑ *Penalty: Yellow*—A player who commits illegal grappling that is either intentional, not immediately adjusted, or in a way that affects gameplay must receive a yellow card.

⚑ *Penalty: Red*—A player who commits grappling in a manner that the referee determines to be violent or egregious conduct must receive a red card.

6.3.2.2. Stealing—A steal consists of a player's attempt to extract a ball from an opponent by either stripping or poking it loose.

A. When to steal: A player may attempt a steal against any opponent of the same position, and keepers and chasers in regard to one another, who is in possession of a ball.

 i. A player may use one or two arms in an attempt to steal as long as neither arm is reaching around the opposing player.

 ii. A player may wrap an opponent with one arm and steal with the other as long as the stealing arm is not reaching around the opponent.

 iii. In an attempt to steal, a player may make initial incidental contact with the player in possession outside of the area generally proscribed under 6.3.1.6.A. This contact does not entitle the player to make other contact with the opponent without releasing and reestablishing contact in accordance with 6.3.1.6.A.

B. Illegal stealing:

 i. A player must not reach over the shoulder or around the neck of an opponent in an attempt to steal the ball.

 ii. A player must not wind up or swing at the ball in an attempt to punch it loose.

 iii. A player must not wrap both arms around an opponent in an attempt to steal. This includes reaching around the opponent with one arm in an attempt to steal while the other arm is being used to wrap the opponent.

⚑ *Penalty: Back to hoops*—A player who commits unintentional illegal physical contact while attempting to steal and immediately adjusts to correct the contact may be sent back to hoops at the discretion of the referee based on whether or not the physical contact affected gameplay.

⚑ *Penalty: Yellow*—A player who commits illegal physical contact while attempting to steal that is either intentional, not immediately adjusted, or in a way that affects gameplay must receive a yellow card.

🏳 *Penalty: Red*—A player who commits illegal contact while attempting to steal in a manner that the referee determines to be violent or egregious conduct must receive a red card.

6.3.2.3. Body blocking—A body block consists of initiating force upon an opponent using body parts other than arms or hands (such as shoulders, chest, or hips). Body blocking is contact that does not use the entire force of the attacking player. In order to be a body block and not a charge, any force initiated must be after non-forceful contact has already been established with the body.

- A. When to body block:
    - i. A player may body block any opponent of the same position, and keepers and chasers in regard to one another, at any point during the game.
    - ii. Hips, shoulders, chest, or any part of a player's torso except the arms (unless the arms are pinned to the torso) may be used in a body block.
    - iii. A player may body block another player running in the same direction as them to gain space or knock the other player off the path.
- B. Illegal body blocking:
    - i. If the initial contact is forceful, the move should be considered a charge and all of the rules regarding charges apply (See: 6.3.2.5. Charging).
    - ii. If force is only applied through the arms (unless pinned to the torso) the move should be considered a push, and all rules regarding pushes apply (See: 6.3.2.4. Pushing).
    - iii. It is illegal to body block using the head, legs, or feet.
    - iv. It is illegal to body block an opponent in the head,

neck, groin, or at or below the knees.

v. A body block must be not be initiated from behind (See: 6.3.1.6. Initial point of contact).

🏴 *Penalty: Back to hoops*—A player who commits an unintentional illegal body block and immediately adjusts to correct the contact may be sent back to hoops at the discretion of the referee based on whether or not the physical contact affected gameplay.

🏴 *Penalty: Yellow*—A player who commits an illegal body block that is either intentional, not immediately adjusted, or in a way that affects gameplay must receive a yellow card.

🏴 *Penalty: Red*—A player who commits an illegal body block in a manner that the referee determines to be violent or egregious conduct must receive a red card.

6.3.2.4. Pushing—A push consists of initiating force upon an opponent with an extended arm, be it extended during or before initiation of contact.

- A. When to push—A player may push any opponent of the same position, and keepers and chasers in regard to one another, at any point during the game.
    - i. Only one arm may be used to push.
    - ii. A push must not be initiated from behind (See: 6.3.1.6. Initial point of contact).
- B. Illegal pushing:
    - i. A push becomes illegal when it becomes a charge directed at an opponent who is not in possession of a ball, unless the player initiating the push is in possession of a ball (See: 6.3.2.5. Charging).
    - ii. It is illegal to push using the head, elbow, or feet.

iii. It is illegal to push with two arms or hands.

iv. It is illegal to push an opponent in the head, neck, groin, or at or below the knees.

v. A push must be not be initiated from behind (See: 6.3.1.6. Initial point of contact).

vi. It is illegal to push a helpless receiver.

🏴 *Penalty: Back to hoops*—A player who commits unintentional illegal pushing and immediately adjusts to correct the contact may be sent back to hoops at the discretion of the referee based on whether or not the physical contact affected gameplay.

🏴 *Penalty: Yellow*—A player who commits illegal pushing that is either intentional, not immediately adjusted, or in a way that affects gameplay must receive a yellow card.

🏴 *Penalty: Red*—A player who commits illegal pushing in a manner that the referee determines to be violent or egregious conduct must receive a red card.

6.3.2.5. Charging—A charge consists of turning or launching your body directly at an opponent and forcefully bumping into them so as to halt their progress, knock them off balance, or knock them to the ground.

A. When to charge:

i. A player without possession of a ball may charge any opponent of the same position, and keepers and chasers in regard to one another, who is in complete and sole possession of a ball.

ii. A player with possession of a ball may charge any opponent of the same position, and keepers and chasers in regard to one another.

B. Illegal charging:
   i. It is illegal to charge an opponent who is not in complete and sole possession of a ball unless the player charging has possession of a ball.
   ii. It is illegal to initiate contact during a charge so that a single point of the charging player's body initiates the contact of the charge, such as leading with the point of a shoulder or leading with an elbow. However, side to side or point-of-shoulder to point-of-shoulder contact is permissible.
   iii. It is illegal for a charging player's feet to leave the ground during a charge.
   iv. It is illegal to charge an opponent in the head, neck, groin, or at or below the knees.
   v. A charge must be not be initiated from behind (See: 6.3.1.6. Initial point of contact).
   vi. It is illegal to charge a helpless receiver.

🏳 *Penalty: Back to hoops*—A player who commits unintentional illegal charging and immediately adjusts to correct the contact may be sent back to hoops at the discretion of the referee based on whether or not the physical contact affected gameplay.

🏳 *Penalty: Yellow*—A player who commits illegal charging that is either intentional, not immediately adjusted, or in a way that affects gameplay must receive a yellow card.

🏳 *Penalty: Red*—A player who commits illegal charging in a manner that the referee determines to be violent or egregious conduct must receive a red card.

6.3.2.6. Grabbing—A grab consists of holding an opponent or any part of an opponent with a closed hand.

   A. When to grab:
       i. A player may grab any opponent of the same position, and keepers and chasers in regard to one another, with possession of a ball.
      ii. Only one hand may be used to grab.
     iii. A player may cause their opponent to dismount through an otherwise legal grab.
   B. Illegal grabbing:
       i. It is illegal to grab an opponent who is not in possession of a ball.
      ii. It is illegal to grab an opponent's broom or clothing.
     iii. It is illegal to grab an opponent in the head, neck, groin, or at or below the knees.
     iv. A grab must be not be initiated from behind (See: 6.3.1.6. Initial point of contact).
      v. It is illegal to pull or yank an opponent during a grab.

⚑ *Penalty: Back to hoops*—A player who commits unintentional illegal grabbing and immediately adjusts to correct the contact may be sent back to hoops at the discretion of the referee based on whether or not the physical contact affected gameplay.

⚑ *Penalty: Yellow*—A player who commits illegal grabbing that is either intentional, not immediately adjusted, or in a way that affects gameplay must receive a yellow card.

⚑ *Penalty: Red*—A player who commits illegal grabbing in a manner that the referee determines to be violent or egregious conduct must receive a red card.

6.3.2.7. Wrapping—A wrap consists of encircling an opponent's torso, or any part of an opponent, with an arm or arms.

- A. When to wrap:
    - i. A player may wrap any opponent of the same position, and keepers and chasers in regard to one another, with possession of a ball.
    - ii. Only one arm may be used to wrap an opponent.
- B. Illegal wrapping:
    - i. It is illegal to wrap an opponent who is not in possession of a ball.
    - ii. It is illegal to wrap an opponent using both arms.
    - iii. It is illegal to wrap an opponent around the neck, head, groin, or at or below the knee.
    - iv. A wrap must be not be initiated from behind (See: 6.3.1.6. Initial point of contact).
    - v. It is illegal to wrap a helpless receiver.

⚑ *Penalty: Back to hoops*—A player who commits unintentional illegal wrapping contact and immediately adjusts to correct the contact may be sent back to hoops at the discretion of the referee based on whether or not the physical contact affected gameplay.

⚑ *Penalty: Yellow*—A player who commits illegal wrapping that is either intentional, not immediately adjusted, or in a way that affects gameplay must receive a yellow card.

⚑ *Penalty: Red*—A player who commits illegal wrapping in a manner that the referee determines to be violent or egregious conduct must receive a red card.

6.3.2.8. Tackling—The act of wrapping a player and bringing the player to the ground.

A. When to tackle:
   i. A player may tackle any opponent of the same position, and keepers and chasers in regard to one another, with possession of a ball.
   ii. Only one arm may be used to tackle an opponent.
B. Illegal tackling:
   i. It is illegal to tackle an opponent who is not in possession of a ball.
   ii. It is illegal to tackle an opponent using both arms.
   iii. It is illegal for a player to leave the ground during a tackle in an attempt to spear or otherwise propel the tackler's body into an opponent.
   iv. It is illegal to tackle an opponent around the neck, head, or groin, or at or below the knee.
   v. It is illegal to complete a tackle that was initiated from behind (See: 6.3.1.6. Initial point of contact).
   vi. It is illegal to tackle a helpless receiver.
C. Completing a tackle:
   i. Once a tackle has been initiated legally, the tackler may continue the already initiated motion of the tackle due to momentum even if the player being tackled releases the ball.
      a. The referee must shout "ball out" the moment the ball is released.
   ii. Extension of the tackle beyond that is illegal contact.
D. Safe tackling:
   i. Players are encouraged and expected to learn and utilize safe tackling techniques, including ensuring that the tackler's head is firmly on one side of the body, head is up, arm is wrapped, etc.

🏴 *Penalty: Back to hoops*—A player who commits unintentional illegal tackling and immediately adjusts to correct the contact may be sent back to hoops at the discretion of the referee based on whether or not the physical contact affected gameplay.

🏴 *Penalty: Yellow*—A player who commits illegal tackling that is either intentional, not immediately adjusted, or in a way that affects gameplay must receive a yellow card.

🏴 *Penalty: Red*—A player who commits illegal tackling in a manner that the referee determines to be violent or egregious conduct must receive a red card.

6.3.3. Interposition right of way

Players of different positions may not physically interact with each other, except for keepers and chasers with regard to each other. The following rules apply to these interactions:

A. The following is the order of priority for right of way between two players of different positions from highest to lowest priority:
   i. A stationary player with a ball.
   ii. A stationary chaser/keeper without a ball.
   iii. A moving player with a ball.
   iv. A stationary beater or seeker without a ball.
   v. A moving player without a ball.
B. Players with lower priority must yield to players with higher priority.
   i. If a player is running at an opposing player over whom they hold priority, the opposing player must make all reasonable efforts to get out of the way.
   ii. If a player of lower priority fails to yield, resulting in

contact, or forcing the player of higher priority to yield to avoid contact, the player who failed to yield shall be deemed "at fault" for that illegal interaction.

C. When two players of the same priority interact, the player whom the referee judges to be at fault for the interaction shall be deemed "at fault."

    i. If the players are judged to be equally at fault for the interaction, no penalty shall be given.

D. If a player with a higher priority clearly acts with the intent of causing an illegal interpositional interaction, that player shall be deemed "at fault," despite their priority.

E. If an offensive player moves with the intent of causing a defender to enter an illegal interpositional interaction with or yield to another player of equal or higher priority, that offensive player shall be deemed "at fault" rather than either of the interacting parties.

F. If the referee determines that there was not enough time for the "at fault" player to reasonably react and yield, the interaction shall be deemed incidental, and no penalty shall be given.

    i. This provision shall not activate as a result of a player's lack of awareness of their surroundings.

🏳 *Penalty: Back to hoops*—A player who is "at fault" for an illegal interpositional interaction but was judged to be unaware of the player with whom they interacted may be sent back to hoops at the discretion of the referee based on whether or not the interaction affected gameplay.

🏳 *Penalty: Yellow*—A player who is "at fault" for an illegal interpositional interaction that is either intentional or affects gameplay must receive a yellow card.

▶ *Penalty: Red*—A player who commits an illegal interpositional interaction in a manner that the referee determines to be violent or egregious conduct must receive a red card.

7. Players

7.1. TEAM COMPOSITION

7.1.1. Rosters and players

A. Each team is made up of at least seven players and no more than 21 players.

   i. Prior to the seeker floor ending, a maximum of one keeper, two beaters, and three chasers (a total of six players) from each team may be in play. After the seeker floor ends, a maximum of one keeper, two beaters, three chasers, and one seeker (a total of seven players) from each team may be in play.

   ii. A team must have seven eligible players to begin a game.

   a. If, over the course of a game, the team no longer has seven eligible players, the game may continue with fewer than seven players.

   b. One keeper, one beater, and one chaser are compulsory in play, even when there are fewer than seven players.

      1. This includes players in the penalty box.

      2. After 18 minutes of game time, a seeker is also required, although no penalty shall be given for lacking a seeker if the seeker is unintentionally late in reporting, so long as there is a substitute who is eligible to fill the role.

    c. If a team is reduced to having fewer than four eligible players at any time during a game, that team must forfeit the game.

B. Team rosters must abide by all USQ regulations regarding rosters.

🚩 *Penalty*—If the referee determines that a team is intentionally failing to send a seeker into the game, the speaking captain must be given a yellow card.

7.1.2. Speaking captains

7.1.2.1. Mandatory speaking captain—Each team must designate one individual to serve as the speaking captain for a game.

A. Only the speaking captain has the power to speak for the team when conversing with officials.

B. The speaking captain may speak with the referees at any time unless the referee asks the speaking captain to stop.

C. The speaking captain may step onto the pitch to talk to a referee, even when not in play, but may not interfere with play in any way.

D. Each team must select an alternate speaking captain if the team's speaking captain is unable to continue the duties of the position for any reason.

🚩 *Penalty: General*—If the speaking captain engages in any action, other than stepping onto the pitch, that would result in a card for a substitute, the speaking captain must receive the same card.

🚩 *Penalty: Blue*—If a speaking captain unintentionally interferes with play while on the pitch and not in play, the speaking captain must receive a blue card.

🏳 *Penalty: Yellow*—If a speaking captain continues conversing with a referee after the referee has asked them to stop, or otherwise ignores a referee's instruction, the speaking captain must receive a yellow card.

🏳 *Penalty: Yellow*—If a member of the opposing team targets the speaking captain while the speaking captain is on the field and not in play, in an attempt to draw a card for speaking captain interference, that player must receive a yellow card, and the speaking captain shall receive no penalty.

🏳 *Penalty: Red*—If the speaking captain intentionally interferes with play while on the pitch and not in play, the speaking captain must receive a red card.

7.1.2.2. Speaking captain eligibility:

A. The team may designate either a player or non-player as the speaking captain.
   i. Any person designated as the speaking captain must be on the team's official roster as either a player or a coach.
   ii. If the speaking captain is not on the roster as a player, the speaking captain must never enter the game as a player.
   iii. A team's speaking captain is not required to be the person who has undergone USQ coach certification, but the USQ certified coach may be designated as the speaking captain or may serve as the speaking captain if no other speaking captain is designated.
B. Only one person may serve as a team's designated speaking captain at any given time.

    i. The speaking captain designation may not be passed from one individual to another during a game unless and until the designated speaking captain is forced to leave the player area, either by injury, penalty, or while tending to another injured teammate.

7.1.2.3. If the team's speaking captain or any non-playing rostered team member receives a penalty while not in active gameplay:

A. If a non-playing rostered member of a team receives a blue or yellow card:
    i. The speaking captain must select a player currently in active gameplay to serve the penalty time and the non-player and that player must both report to the penalty box.

B. If the speaking captain or any non-playing rostered team member receives a red card while not in active gameplay:
    i. The person who received the red card is ejected from the game.
    ii. If the speaking captain receives a red card, the alternate speaking captain must assume the duties of the speaking captain.
    iii. The speaking captain (or alternate, if the speaking captain is ejected) selects a player currently in active gameplay to serve the two minutes of penalty time for the red card.

7.1.3. Gender maximum rule

A quidditch game allows each team to have a maximum of four players who identify as the same gender in active play on the field at the same time. This number increases to five once the seekers enter the game.

A. Prior to the expiration of the seeker floor in the current period of the game, a team may not have more than four players who identify as the same gender in play.

B. Upon the expiration of the seeker floor, a team may not have more than five players who identify as the same gender in play.

    i. A team may not have five players who identify as the same gender in play until the initial seeker enters play.

    ii. A player serving penalty time is considered in play.

C. The gender that a player identifies with is considered to be that player's gender.

D. In the event that a team cannot field a full team as fielding a full team would cause that team to exceed the gender maximum due to injury or ejection, the team may continue to play with fewer than six (or seven if after the seeker floor has ended) players, with the missing player(s) not counting toward the gender maximum.

    i. The teams must still have one player in play at each position (See: 7.1.1.A.ii.b.).

🏴 *Penalty: Special*—If there is ever an illegal player or set of players in play, in terms of eligibility, gender, number of players, or position, the referee must stop play and the offending team must correct the illegal situation. The team's speaking captain must receive a yellow card.

7.2. GENERAL PLAYER RULES

7.2.1. General principle

A player may take any action that does not violate the rules.

7.2.2. Using the balls

7.2.2.1. Players may possess touch, kick, throw, or otherwise use the ball associated with their own position. Possession is defined as when a player has complete and sole control of a ball. The following guidelines apply:

A. Players may only possess, touch, kick, throw, or otherwise use one ball associated with their position at any given time that they are in active gameplay.

B. Players may not use the ball associated with their position to mimic the actions of the ball of a different position.

> *7.2.2.1.B. Example: A chaser may not intentionally throw the quaffle at an opponent as if it were a bludger. A beater may not intentionally throw a bludger through the hoops as if it were a quaffle, unless the beater is throwing the bludger through the hoop in order to attempt to make a knockout, pass, or to hit the quaffle.* .

C. Players may not use a ball of their position to intentionally interact with the snitch runner.

📖 *Penalty: Blue*—A player who uses a ball to mimic the actions of a ball of a different position must receive a blue card.

📖 *Penalty: Blue*—A player who uses a possessed or propelled ball with the intent of interacting with the snitch runner must receive a blue card.

7.2.2.2. Players are forbidden from possessing, touching, kicking, throwing, or in any way using the ball of another position. The following guidelines apply:

A. Any mounted player who may not play the quaffle, must take any and all reasonable actions to avoid a propelled quaffle.

    i. If a beater stands in the quaffle's way and throws their bludger at the quaffle in an attempt to deflect it but is hit by the quaffle despite the attempt, they are still penalized.

    ii. A player shall not be penalized for an interaction with the quaffle if, at the discretion of the referee, they were not aware of the incoming quaffle, unless the referee also determines that they intentionally acted so as to be unaware.

    iii. A player shall not be penalized for an interaction with the quaffle if, at the discretion of the referee, there was not enough time for the player to reasonably react and yield; the interaction shall be deemed incidental and no penalty shall be given.

    iv. This rule does not prohibit a beater from throwing or propelling a bludger at the quaffle.

B. Any mounted player who may not play a bludger, may allow a live bludger to hit them, or intentionally get in the way of a live bludger for any reason, as long as that bludger was initially propelled by an opponent.

    i. A player may allow the bludger to bounce off of any part of their body or equipment at any angle. However they must not propel the bludger in any direction.

        a. Any attempt to bat away, swat, or otherwise intentionally propel a live bludger during an initial hit to a player is considered a bludger swat.

1. A referee may choose to call no harm no foul on a bludger swat if the propulsion was minor and did not affect overall play or bludger possession. However, if a single player is repeatedly committing minor swatting in a match, that player should be penalized regardless of the outcome of the swats.

2. If the referee determines that a player moved into the path of a bludger with the intent to illegally swat it, that action must be ruled as intentionally illegally interacting with a ball of another position.

b. This rule does not prohibit a chaser or keeper from using a held quaffle to swat a live bludger or from throwing a quaffle at a live bludger.

ii. If the referee determines that the player was not reasonably aware that the airborne bludger was either dead, or made live by their own teammate, and the play was otherwise legal, the player shall not be penalized.

iii. If an immune keeper moves so as to intentionally be hit by a bludger which would not otherwise have contacted them, they shall be subject to the knockout effect upon contact with that live bludger, as though they were not immune.

🏴 *Penalty: Back to hoops*—A player who attempts to avoid a propelled quaffle that they must avoid, but fails to successfully avoid contact with it, may be sent back to hoops at the discretion of the referee based on whether or not the interaction affected gameplay.

🏴 *Penalty: Blue*—A player who illegally interacts with a quaffle by failing to attempt to avoid it or in a way that affects gameplay must receive a blue card.

🏴 *Penalty: Blue*—A player who illegally swats a bludger must receive a blue card.

🏴 *Penalty: Yellow*—A player who intentionally illegally interacts with ball of another position must receive a yellow card.

🏴 *Penalty: Yellow*—A player who illegally interacts with a propelled quaffle in a way that blocks a score must receive a yellow card.

🏴 *Penalty: Red*—A player who illegally and intentionally blocks the quaffle from scoring must receive a red card, except in cases of goaltending as described in 4.3. Goaltending.

7.2.2.3. A substitute must make a reasonable effort, at the referee's discretion, not to interact with any ball.

7.2.2.4. A knocked out player must make a reasonable effort, at the referee's discretion, not to interact with any ball.

🏴 *Penalty: Yellow*—A substitute or knocked out player who does not make a reasonable effort to avoid interacting with a ball in play, at the discretion of the referee, must receive a yellow card.

🏴 *Penalty: Red*—A substitute or knocked out player who illegally and intentionally blocks a score must receive a red card.

7.2.3. Boundaries and players

7.2.3.1. All play must occur within the player area.

🏴 *Penalty: Blue*—A player who illegally leaves the player area to make a play must receive a blue card.

7.2.3.2. Play confined to the pitch—A player who leaves the pitch must return to it, except under the following conditions:

A. Once the seekers have entered the game, a seeker may leave the pitch in pursuit of the snitch runner, including trying to gain possession of a snitch near the pitch boundary, or to block the opposing seeker.
   i. Neither the snitch runner nor the seekers may leave the player area.
B. Any player may leave the pitch boundary to directly pursue a ball that they are eligible to possess that is beyond the boundary.
   i. If a ball exits the player area, the proper eligible player may retrieve the ball with explicit permission of any referee, or if not stopped by a referee while the closest eligible player attempting to retrieve a bludger.
C. Any player may leave the pitch boundary to defend against an opponent in possession of a ball that is beyond the boundary.
D. Any player physically forced beyond the pitch boundary is not subject to penalty.
   i. The player should return to the pitch as directly and immediately as possible.
E. A beater in possession of a bludger may leave the pitch boundary in order to pursue any opponent eligible to be knocked out who is off of the pitch.
F. If a player's forward progress is contested near the pitch boundary, with or without physical contact, the player is allowed to cross over the pitch boundary to circumvent the defender.

    i. After crossing the boundary, the player must, at the referee's discretion, directly and immediately return to the pitch.

    ii. Once off the pitch while circumventing an opponent, the player may not alter their path to angle further away from the pitch, unless forced to do so through direct physical contact.

        a. If an opponent blocks the player's path off the pitch, the player must either proceed through the opponent (if this is otherwise legal), circumvent the opponent by cutting back in towards the pitch, or retreat back onto the pitch.

⚑ *Penalty: Back to hoops*—A player who illegally and intentionally leaves the pitch or remains off of the pitch must be sent back to hoops.

⚑ *Penalty: Back to hoops*—A player who illegally alters their path to angle further away from the pitch while off pitch must be sent back to hoops.

7.2.4. Boundaries and balls

7.2.4.1. A player may not intentionally propel a ball out of the player area.

7.2.4.2. A player may not intentionally distance a ball from the pitch except under the following circumstances:

    A. A beater may carry a bludger off pitch while pursuing an opponent who is off the pitch.

    B. A player may distance a ball from the pitch if the player does so while attempting to score, complete a pass to a player on the pitch, or knock out an opponent, at the discretion of the referee.

C. A player may carry a ball with them while legally leaving the pitch under rules 7.2.3.2.D-F.

D. A beater may propel a bludger which was already off pitch further off pitch in an attempt to knock out an opponent.

E. A keeper may propel the quaffle in a way that would be illegal for other players while making a save in their own keeper zone.

⚑ *Penalty: Back to hoops*—A player who illegally and intentionally carries a ball off or away from the pitch must be sent back to hoops.

⚑ *Penalty: Back to hoops and turnover*—A player who illegally propels a ball off the pitch, laterally from the pitch, or further away from the pitch while off the pitch must receive receive a back to hoops and the ball is turned over to the closest eligible player of the opposing team to the location of the ball at the end of the play.

⚑ *Penalty: Yellow*—A player who intentionally carries a ball out of the player area, or propels a ball with the intent of sending it out of the player area, must receive a yellow card.

7.2.5. The spectator area

7.2.5.1. Any area outside of the player area is the spectator area. No play may occur in the spectator area.

A. Players may not physically force another player into the spectator area.

B. Players may not initiate contact inside the spectator area.

C. Players may not step out of the player area unless retrieving a ball.

    i. If a the quaffle carrier illegally contacts the ground on or outside of the player area boundary, without being forced out by an opponent, the quaffle shall be considered out as well.

🚩 *Penalty: Back to hoops*—A player who illegally contacts the ground on or outside of the player area boundary without being physically forced must be sent back to hoops.

🚩 *Penalty: Yellow*—A player who physically forces another player into the spectator area or who initiates contact with a player while outside of the player area must receive a yellow card.

🚩 *Penalty: Red*—A player who initiates contact with another player while outside of the player area in a manner that the referee determines to be violent or egregious conduct must receive a red card.

7.2.5.2. Players may not enter the spectator area unless allowed to do so by a referee under one or more of the following conditions:

A. If the quaffle enters the spectator area and play is not stopped:

    i. The head referee signals verbally and visually which team is eligible to retrieve the quaffle and a player from that team may do so.

    ii. The quaffle shall be awarded to the nearest eligible player on the team that did not last touch the quaffle.

    iii. The player retrieving the quaffle shall bring it back directly and immediately crossing, if possible, the point where it went out of the player area.

       iv. The defending team must allow the player to return to the player area before moving to defend at the point where the player shall return.

B. If the quaffle enters the spectator area in any of the following circumstances, play must be stopped and any player, official, or spectator may retrieve the quaffle at the directive of the head referee:

       i. If, at the discretion of the referee, the quaffle has gone too far from the player area.

       ii. Retrieval may unnecessarily delay the game.

       iii. Retrieval may be dangerous for players or spectators.

       iv. A keeper made a save in their own keeper zone.

C. If the quaffle goes out of the player area and play is stopped:

       i. The quaffle shall be awarded to the nearest eligible player on the team that did not last touch the quaffle at a location approximately two feet inside where it left the player area, except in cases covered in 7.2.5.2.C.ii.

       ii. If a keeper made a save in their own keeper zone, at the discretion of the referee, and the quaffle leaves the player area, the quaffle is awarded to that keeper.

D. If a bludger enters the spectator area, play continues.

       i. The nearest eligible beater, from either team, may enter the spectator area to retrieve the bludger, unless stopped by a referee.

       ii. If there are beaters from both teams pursuing the bludger:

          a. A referee must indicate the appropriate player to retrieve the bludger.

          b. The other player must abandon pursuit of the bludger and must allow the opposing player to clearly return to the player area before beginning any interaction.

iii. If there are no players in pursuit of the bludger:
   a. The bludger must be retrieved by a referee.
   b. The bludger must be set at a location approximately two feet inside the point where it left the player area.
   c. The bludger may then be retrieved by any eligible beater on either team.
E. A player is in need of medical attention (See: 2.1.8.2. The spectator area).

|◣ *Penalty: Yellow*—A player who disregards a referee's instruction regarding entering the spectator area must receive a yellow card.

7.2.6. Spectators and dangerous terrain

7.2.6.1. There must be no dangerous terrain within the player area.

7.2.6.2. Play must be stopped whenever players are at risk of contacting spectators or dangerous terrain, at the discretion of the head referee.

A. If play must be stopped for one of these reasons, any player with a ball resumes where they were when play was stopped.
   i. If no player possesses the relevant ball at the time of the stoppage, the ball is given to the closest eligible player.
B. Any other players must move back to the pitch boundary, at the closest point to where they were when play was stopped.
   i. Once play is restarted they may leave the pitch boundary to pursue the player with possession of the ball.

|◣ *Penalty: Yellow*—A player who recklessly endangers a spectator must receive a yellow card.

7.2.7. Playing recklessly

It is illegal to play recklessly. This includes playing with complete disregard for danger to opponents or to spectators.

🚩 *Penalty: Yellow*—A player who plays recklessly at any time, at the discretion of the referee, must receive a yellow card.

🚩 *Penalty: Red*—A player who participates in particularly egregious reckless play must receive a red card.

7.3. QUAFFLE PLAYER RULES

7.3.1. The quaffle players are the three chasers and one keeper on each team.

7.3.1.1. Chaser overview—See: 1.2.1. Chaser overview.

7.3.1.2. Keeper overview—See: 1.2.2. Keeper overview.

7.3.2. Using the quaffle

Chasers and keepers may touch, carry, pass, kick, and take shots at the goal with the quaffle.

7.3.2.1. Scoring with the quaffle:

 A. Quaffle players may throw, kick, pass or in any legal way make the quaffle travel through a hoop to score a goal.
 B. Quaffle players may take shots at the goals from anywhere within the player area.
 C. Any part of the quaffle player's body may accompany the quaffle through the hoops.
 D. Quaffle players may score from either side of the hoop.

7.3.2.2. Kicking the quaffle:

 A. Quaffle players, except for protected keepers, are only

allowed to kick the quaffle once.

B. After the quaffle has been kicked by a player, except for a protected keeper, it must then be picked up by any player before that player is allowed to kick it again.

7.3.2.3. Blocking bludgers with the quaffle:

A. Quaffle players may use the quaffle, and only the quaffle, to block incoming bludgers.

B. If they are successful and are not hit anywhere on their bodies or brooms, including the hand holding the quaffle, then the deflection is complete and the bludger has no effect, even if the quaffle is dropped during the deflection.

   i. If the bludger bounces off the held quaffle and subsequently hits the blocking player or their broom before it becomes dead, the knockout effect is still incurred as normal.

C. A quaffle player may use the quaffle to bat, swat, or otherwise propel a live bludger away with the quaffle in an attempt to block a knockout.

   i. A quaffle player without a quaffle may not bat, swat, or otherwise propel a live bludger (See: 5.2.6. Swatting bludgers).

D. A quaffle player may not intentionally interact with a dead bludger, including a bludger that is still in the hand of a beater.

   i. A held quaffle may not be used to interact with a dead bludger.

   ii. A quaffle may not be thrown at a dead bludger.

   iii. A quaffle player without a quaffle may not interact with a dead bludger.

E. A quaffle may be thrown at a live bludger.

🏴 *Penalty: Blue*—A quaffle player who uses the quaffle illegally must receive a blue card.

🏴 *Penalty: Turnover*—If a quaffle player unintentionally acts on a bludger in a manner that significantly affects the position of the bludger, the bludger must be turned over to the closest eligible beater of the opposing team.

🏴 *Penalty: Yellow*—A quaffle player who intentionally interacts with a bludger illegally must receive a yellow card.

7.3.3. Keeper-specific rules

7.3.3.1. While outside the keeper zone the keeper is subject to all of the same rules as a chaser, including but not limited to the knockout effect.

    A. A player with any part of their body behind or touching their own keeper zone line is considered to be in the keeper zone.

    B. Once the offensive team possesses the quaffle outside the keeper zone:

        i. The keeper loses all powers of a protected keeper listed under 7.3.3.2.

       ii. The powers listed in 7.3.3.2. are regained after the opposing team gains possession of the quaffle, a goal is scored, or the period ends.

7.3.3.2. Keeper-specific powers—A keeper within their own keeper zone, except in the situation described in 7.3.3.1.B., is considered to be a protected keeper. A protected keeper is subject to all of the same rules as a chaser with the following exceptions:

    A. If a protected keeper kicks the quaffle in their own keeper zone, it is not counted as a kick by that player. A protected keeper may kick the quaffle any number of times while in their own keeper zone.

B.   Once a protected keeper has sole possession of the quaffle, opposing players may not contact, interact with, or attempt to steal the quaffle from the keeper (See: 6.3.1.2. Illegal physical contact).

   i.   Sole possession of the quaffle must be established before this immunity from contact goes into effect.

C.   A protected keeper is immune to the knockout effect.

   i.   There is no penalty for beaters throwing bludgers at immune players.

D.   A protected keeper is allowed to block a shot in a way that would be considered goaltending for any other player (See: 4.3. Goaltending).

E.   If a protected keeper saves a shot and the quaffle goes into the spectator area, the keeper is granted possession rather than the other team (See: 7.2.5.2.C).

7.3.3.3. Keeper restart—After a goal has been scored, the quaffle is dead until quaffle play is restarted as soon as the keeper has possession of the quaffle subject to all regulations in 4.4.2. Dead quaffle and 4.4.3. Keeper restart.

7.4. BEATER RULES

7.4.1. Beater overview

See: 1.2.3. Beater overview.

7.4.2. Using the bludger

Beaters may touch, pass, carry, kick, or throw any bludger but may only be in contact with one bludger at any given time (not including being hit by a thrown bludger while they are holding another bludger).

7.4.2.1. The knockout effect—Beaters may throw, kick, or in any way propel the bludgers to disrupt the flow of the game by "knocking out" other players (See: 5.2. The knockout effect).

7.4.2.2. Kicking a bludger:

A. After a bludger has been kicked by a player, it must then be picked up before they are allowed to kick it again.
B. Even if the beater incurs the knockout effect on an opponent with a kick, then they may not kick it again until it has been picked up.
C. A beater may not kick a bludger while in possession of a second bludger.

🏴 *Penalty: Blue*—A beater who performs an illegal second kick to a bludger must receive a blue card.

7.4.2.3. Catching a bludger:

A. Beaters may catch bludgers that are thrown at them by opposing players.
  i. If the catch causes the beater to have possession of two bludgers, one must immediately be dropped to avoid penalty.
B. If a beater catches a thrown bludger, the knockout effect does not occur and the beater may continue play as normal.
C. Any teammates hit by the bludger before it was caught are still knocked out.
D. A caught ball has no effect on the thrower. See: 5.2.4.

Struck beater for additional regulations regarding attempting to catch bludgers to negate the knockout effect.

7.4.2.4. Deflecting/blocking a bludger:

A. Beaters may use a bludger to block incoming bludgers.
B. If a beater is successful and is not hit anywhere on their body, including the hand holding the bludger, then the deflection is complete and the bludger has no effect, even if a bludger is dropped during the deflection.
   i. If the incoming bludger bounces off the held bludger and subsequently hits the blocking player or their broom before it becomes dead, the knockout effect is still incurred as normal.
C. A beater may use their bludger to bat, swat, or otherwise propel a live bludger away with their bludger in an attempt to block a knockout.
   i. A beater with a bludger may not swat, or otherwise propel a live bludger on first contact, unless they are swatting it with their held bludger.
   ii. A beater without a bludger may swat or otherwise propel a live bludger on first contact, but the bludger remains live for the original team and the swatting beater is knocked out.
D. Using a held bludger to knowingly and intentionally interact with a dead bludger, or one that is still in the possession of an opponent, is an illegal interaction.

🏴 *Penalty: Blue*—A beater who interacts with a bludger illegally must receive a blue card.

7.4.2.5. Possession of bludgers and interactions with the quaf-

fle:

A. A player is considered to have possession of a bludger when that player has sole and complete control of that bludger. This includes when a player is the only player in contact with the bludger during a swat or a kick.

B. Except in the circumstance described in 7.4.2.5.C., a beater may only be in possession of one bludger at a time.

C. A beater may temporarily possess two bludgers if the beater is in the process of catching a live bludger propelled by an opponent.

    i. In this scenario, the beater must drop one of the two bludgers immediately to avoid penalty.

       a. Throwing or otherwise propelling this bludger, rather than dropping it, shall result in a penalty for possessing more than one bludger.

D. A beater must not possess or intentionally interact with the quaffle, other than throwing a bludger at the quaffle.

🏴 *Penalty: Blue*—A beater who possesses two bludgers at one time while not trying to catch a bludger, or who does not drop one bludger immediately after possessing two during a catch, must receive a blue card.

🏴 *Penalty: Turnover*—If a beater unintentionally acts on a quaffle in a manner that significantly affects the position of the quaffle, the quaffle must be turned over to the closest eligible player of the opposing team.

🏴 *Penalty: Yellow*—A beater who possesses or intentionally interacts with a quaffle illegally must receive a yellow card.

7.4.2.6. Guarding bludgers—Guarding a bludger is defined as taking any action that would prevent or significantly delay the opposing team from gaining possession of a bludger.

A. A team in possession of one bludger may guard a second bludger.

B. A team in possession of two bludgers may not guard the remaining bludger, even if the opposing team does not request immunity.

C. It is considered guarding if either of the beaters on a team with two bludgers:

    i. Throws one of the bludgers that had been in their team's possession in any direction other than toward the opposing team's hoops, unless attempting to knock out an opposing player, and then takes possession of the bludger that was free beforehand.

    ii. Continually or intentionally moves into the path of an opponent attempting to gain possession of the free bludger so as to delay or hinder the ability of the opponent to reach the ball.

    iii. Relinquishes control of a bludger in hand by releasing it directly to the ground and then takes control of the free bludger.

    iv. Makes a clear effort to prevent the opposition from gaining possession of the bludger, at discretion of the referee, in accordance with 7.4.2.6.D.

D. It is not considered guarding if either of the beaters on a team with two bludgers:

    i. Throws a possessed bludger at an opponent in an attempt to knock an opponent out of the game and then takes control of the free bludger.

    ii. Relinquishes control of a bludger to the opposing

team by throwing the bludger in the direction of the opposing team's hoops.

iii. Attempts to knock out the beater recovering the third bludger if the recovering beater has not claimed knockout immunity.

🏳 *Penalty: Back to hoops*—A player who, at the discretion of the referee, is guarding the free bludger while the player's team is in possession of two bludgers must be sent back to hoops.

7.4.3. Knockout immunity

In certain situations, beaters may become immune to the knockout effect by raising a closed fist (See: 5.2.8. Knockout immunity).

7.4.4. Bludger vs. quaffle

7.4.4.1. Beaters may not use a bludger they are holding to affect the trajectory of the quaffle.

7.4.4.2. Beaters may throw or kick a bludger at the quaffle.

🏳 *Penalty: Turnover*—A beater unintentionally acting on a quaffle with a held bludger, in a manner that significantly affects the position or trajectory of the quaffle, results in a turnover of the quaffle to the closest eligible quaffle player of the opposing team.

🏳 *Penalty: Yellow*—A player who, at the discretion of the referee, intentionally uses a held bludger to affect the trajectory of the quaffle must receive a yellow card.

7.5. SEEKER RULES

7.5.1. Seeker overview

See: 1.2.4. Seeker overview.

7.5.2. Catching the snitch

7.5.2.1. The seeker attempts to gain possession of the snitch by removing it from the snitch runner.

7.5.2.2. For a snitch catch to be successful, all circumstances of 4.5. The snitch catch must be met and sole possession of the snitch must be clear and confirmed.

7.5.3. Seeker interactions

7.5.3.1. Seeker interactions with other positions:

A. Seekers are subject to the knockout effect and may be knocked out at any time after they are released.
B. Seekers may not interact with or physically contact players of other positions except for incidental contact in the course of fielding their position.
C. Seekers may not use or intentionally touch any game ball besides the snitch.

⚑ *Penalty: Turnover*—If a seeker unintentionally acts on a bludger or quaffle in a manner that significantly affects the position of the ball, then the ball must be turned over to the closest eligible player on the opposing team to the point of the foul.

⚑ *Penalty: Yellow*—A seeker who intentionally interacts with a bludger or quaffle must receive a yellow card.

7.5.3.2. Seeker interactions with other seekers:

A. Seekers are subject to all physical contact rules and appropriate penalties (See: 6.3. Physical contact).

B. Since seekers are never in possession of a ball while a period is in session, any form of contact that cannot be initiated on a player who is not in possession of a ball is illegal contact for seekers.

7.5.4. Seeker contact with the snitch runner

A seeker may have limited physical contact with the snitch runner. The following guidelines apply:

A. A seeker may push the snitch runner's arms, grapple, body block, or complete other forms of incidental contact with the snitch runner, but this interaction must not limit the snitch runner's mobility.

B. A seeker may not push, grab, hold, charge, wrap, or tackle a snitch runner.

C. A seeker who grabs the snitch runner's clothing must let go immediately to avoid penalty.

   i. Any snitch catch accomplished by, or immediately following, the grabbing of clothing is invalidated.

   ii. If the snitch runner's shorts need to be adjusted, the snitch runner's other clothing obscures the snitch, or the snitch runner's clothing impedes the snitch, the snitch runner must be ruled as down until the clothing has been adjusted.

      a. If the clothing needs to be adjusted, the snitch runner is considered down and the snitch is uncatchable from the moment the clothing is askew, at the discretion of the referee, whether or not the snitch runner or referee has verbalized that the snitch is down.

         1. If this occurs, the snitch shall be considered ruled as down and be given a three second start after

adjusting the clothing.

2. If the clothing is made askew simply because the velcro did not release when holding the snitch sock, 7.5.4.C.ii.a. does not apply.

🏳 *Penalty: Yellow*—A seeker who pushes, grabs, holds, charges, wraps, or tackles the snitch runner, or who does not immediately let go after grabbing the snitch runner's clothing must receive a yellow card.

7.5.5. Seekers during stoppages

Seekers are subject to all stoppages and must stop play immediately when a referee blows the whistle in paired short blasts.

8. Game Officials

8.1. HEAD REFEREE

8.1.1. Authority of the head referee

Each game is controlled by one referee who has full authority to enforce and interpret the rules of the game in connection with the game to which that referee has been appointed. The referee has the authority to take disciplinary action from the moment the referee enters the player area until the referee leaves the player area after the final whistle. Additional officials may be designated and players must follow all directives from those officials as well as the head referee.

8.1.1.1. Players, non-playing team staff, snitch runners, and other officials must defer to the authority of the head referee.

A. Players must abide by the decisions of the head referee and all other officials.

B. Players must not show disrespect to any official or persistently question the decisions of the referees.

🏴 *Penalty: Blue/Yellow*—A player who disrespects an official or persistently questions referees' decisions may receive a blue or yellow card at the discretion of the referee.

🏴 *Penalty: Yellow*—A player who disregards the directives of the head referee must receive a yellow card. Players who disregard the directives of any other official may receive a yellow card at the discretion of the head referee.

8.1.1.2. If assistant referees have not been designated by tournament officials, the head referee must designate at least three additional referees to serve as the assistant and snitch referees.

8.1.2. Powers and duties of the head referee

A. Enforcing the rules of the game.
B. Controlling the game in cooperation with all other officials.
C. Performing all duties of the head referee listed throughout the rulebook.
D. Performing the duties of any officials that are not present.
E. Replacing a snitch runner who is injured or in violation of the rules governing the snitch runner (See: 8.3. The snitch runner).
F. Replacing any official who is injured or, in the opinion of the head referee, needs to be dismissed.
G. Stopping play immediately when a player is too injured to continue play while obstructing active gameplay, or is down with a serious injury. An injured player may only return to the pitch after the game has been resumed.
H. Allowing play to continue if a player appears to be injured but there is no gameplay taking place in the area and the player does not appear to have a serious injury.
I. Ensuring that, when play must be stopped for an injury, the injured player is removed from the pitch.
J. Stopping play to ensure that any player who is openly bleeding leaves the pitch immediately and is replaced by a substitute. The player may only return after receiving permission from an official, who must be satisfied that

the bleeding has stopped.

K. Suspending the game due to cases of severe weather, concerns over safety, extreme or inappropriate misconduct, or external interference.

L. Penalizing the more serious foul when a player commits more than one foul at the same time.

M. Receiving advice, when appropriate, from any relevant officials and making judgements on how to proceed.

N. Indicating the start and end of each period of the game.

O. Reviewing and authorizing official game documents.

P. Having knowledge of the game score at all times and ensuring that it is properly communicated to players, spectators, and other officials, specifically the scorekeeper.

Q. Using verbal and visual commands to communicate with players, other officials, and spectators.

🚩 *Penalty: Blue*—A player who uses verbal or visual referee commands may receive a blue card.

8.1.3. Decisions of the head referee

8.1.3.1. All decisions of the head referee regarding facts connected with play are final. This includes:

A. Determining whether a goal should be counted as good.

B. Issuing any fouls or disciplinary action.

C. Confirming a snitch catch and the final results of the game.

8.1.3.2. Adjusting calls—If the referee has not restarted play, the referee may change a decision upon realizing that the decision was incorrect, or on the advice of another official.

A. Adjusting a goal call:

    i. If a goal was called good by the head referee but evidence arises that the goal was no good, then the referee may adjust the call of the goal at any time prior to a significant interaction or play by the player with possession. Quaffle possession is unaffected by the change.

    ii. If a goal was called no good by the head referee but evidence arises that the goal was good, then the referee may adjust the call of the goal at any time prior to the formerly defending team having possession of the quaffle outside of the keeper zone and a significant interaction or play by the player with possession.

B. Players may not request changes to any decision of a referee.

8.1.3.3. Referee's discretion—In cases where intent or severity are relevant to a call, the referee retains full discretion in judging that severity or intent.

8.2. ASSISTANT REFEREES AND OTHER OFFICIALS

8.2.1. Appointment of assistant referees and other officials

8.2.1.1. The head referee or tournament officials must appoint at least two assistant referees, a snitch referee, and a snitch runner and may appoint other officials (up to two additional assistant referees, a scorekeeper, a timekeeper, and goal judges) for each game.

8.2.1.2. A snitch runner must be appointed for each game.

8.2.1.3. At least two and up to four assistant referees must be appointed.

8.2.1.4. One snitch referee must be appointed. The snitch referee may act as an assistant referee until the snitch runner is released into the player area. The snitch referee must be appointed in addition to the two required assistant referees.

8.2.1.5. It is highly recommended that at least two goal judges, a scorekeeper, and a timekeeper are appointed for each game.

A. If any of these positions is not filled, the head referee assumes the responsibilities of that position.

8.2.2. Assistant referees

8.2.2.1. At least two and up to four assistant referees must be appointed.

8.2.2.2. The duties of the assistant referees, subject to the discretion of the head referee, are:

A. Indicating when a player is subject to the knockout effect.
B. Sending any fouling player back to hoops, then alerting the head referee if a card needs to be issued.
C. Warning beaters who may be guarding the third bludger if their team has possession of two bludgers.
D. Advising the head referee when misconduct or any other incident occurs.
E. Allowing the appropriate beater to retrieve a bludger that has gone into the spectator area or retrieving the bludger and placing it on the edge of the pitch if no eligible beater is available (See: 7.2.5. The spectator area).
F. Watching off-ball quaffle players and ensuring that they are following all rules and regulations.
G. Assisting the head referee with monitoring quaffle play

as necessary.

8.2.2.3. Players must abide by the decisions of any assistant referee.

🏴 *Penalty: Yellow*—A player who disregards the directives of any official may receive a yellow card at the discretion of the head referee.

8.2.3. Snitch referee

8.2.3.1. A snitch referee must be appointed.

    A. The snitch referee may act as an assistant referee until the snitch runner is released into the player area.

8.2.3.2. The duties of the snitch referee, subject to the discretion of the head referee, are:

    A. Stopping play by blowing a whistle in paired short blasts if a snitch catch may have been successful or if the snitch runner or equipment need to be replaced.

    B. Indicating when a snitch runner has been ruled as down and is uncatchable (See: 8.3.9. Ruled as down).

    C. Counting down from three seconds to indicate when the snitch runner is free to be pursued after having been ruled as down (See: 8.3.9. Ruled as down).

    D. Monitoring all interactions between the seekers and the snitch runner and sending any fouling player back to hoops before alerting the head referee if a card needs to be issued.

    E. Ensuring that the snitch runner follows all regulations in section 8.3. The snitch runner.

    F. Ensuring that the snitch runner is informed when the snitch handicaps come into effect.

G. Ensuring that the snitch runner is acting within the confines of the handicaps.

H. Indicating when a player involved in the snitch game (including beaters in the general vicinity of the snitch runner and seekers) is subject to the knockout effect.

8.2.3.3. Players must abide by the decisions of the snitch referee.

🏴 *Penalty: Yellow*—A player who disregards the directives of any official may receive a yellow card at the discretion of the head referee.

8.2.3.4. The snitch referee must not provide any additional advice or warnings to the snitch runner during the game to help them avoid being caught, including but not limited to the locations, substitutions, and tactics of the seekers.

8.2.4. Goal judge

Two goal judges may be appointed. Their duties, subject to the discretion of the head referee, are:

A. Indicating whether a quaffle passing near the hoops is to be ruled as good or no good.

B. Fixing any hoops that are broken or dislodged while play continues, so long as doing so does not interfere with play.

C. Retrieving a dead quaffle (after a goal is scored) if it is out of play, inaccessible to players, or needs to be returned to the keeper.

D. If requested, advising other officials of player fouls, misconduct, or any other incident.

8.2.4.1. Players must abide by the decisions of the goal judges.

🏴 *Penalty: Yellow*—A player who disregards the directives of any official may receive a yellow card at the discretion of the head referee.

8.2.5. Scorekeeper and timekeeper

8.2.5.1. A scorekeeper and a timekeeper may be appointed. One person may be appointed to perform the duties of both the scorekeeper and the timekeeper.

A. The scorekeeper's duties, subject to the discretion of the head referee, are:
   i. Keeping written track of the game's score.
   ii. Updating the game's scoreboard.
   iii. Recording player number and reason for penalty for all blue, yellow, and red cards.
   iv. Announcing the score to teams, officials, and spectators at regular intervals and upon request.
B. The timekeeper's duties, subject to the discretion of the head referee, are:
   i. Stopping the game clock when the head referee stops play (indicated by paired short whistle blasts) and resuming the game clock when the referee has resumed play (indicated by one short whistle blast).
   ii. Keeping track of penalty time and releasing players from the penalty box after their penalty time is served.
   iii. Keeping track of the total game time that the game has lasted, including overtime time if necessary.
   iv. Acknowledging the seekers and snitch runner when they report to the scorekeeper table and releasing them onto the pitch at the appropriate time.
   v. In any overtime period:

a. Announcing the time remaining at regular intervals.
   1. At each minute (four, three, two, and one).
   2. When 30 seconds and 15 seconds remain.
   3. Counting down from ten seconds remaining.
b. Indicating clearly that the period is about to end.
c. Stopping the game clock immediately upon the referee's signal of advantage or delayed penalty.

8.2.5.2. Players must abide by the decisions of the scorekeeper and timekeeper.

🏳 *Penalty: Yellow*—A player who disregards the directives of any official may receive a yellow card at the discretion of the head referee.

8.2.6. The snitch runner as an official

A. The snitch runner may make calls regarding the knockout effect and the legality of the snitch catch if there is no referee present or able to make a call.
B. The snitch runner may offer advice to the snitch referee and the head referee regarding the possible validity of a snitch catch.
C. Players must abide by the decisions of the snitch runner.

🏳 *Penalty: Yellow*—A player who disregards the directives of any official may receive a yellow card at the discretion of the head referee.

8.3. THE SNITCH RUNNER

8.3.1. Role of the snitch runner

8.3.1.1. The role of the snitch runner is to prevent the snitch ball from being caught by either team's seeker for as long as possible, while also serving as a fair and impartial official.

8.3.1.2. The snitch runner's uniform:

   A. The snitch runner must wear shorts with the snitch ball affixed.

      i. The snitch shorts and ball must meet all the requirements in section 2.3.3. The snitch.

   B. The snitch runner must wear a shirt or jersey and be easily identifiable as distinct from either team.

   C. The snitch runner should be dressed in all yellow or gold.

8.3.2. Snitch runner as an official

See: 8.2.6. The snitch runner as an official.

8.3.3. The snitch runner's timing

8.3.3.1. After Brooms Up, the snitch runner should remain in the vicinity of the pitch until the 17 minute mark of game time. During this time:

   A. The snitch ball may not be caught by either team.

   B. The snitch runner may not be within the player area.

   C. The snitch runner may not interfere with play in any manner.

8.3.3.2. At the 17 minute mark of game time, the snitch runner must report to the timekeeper and will be released into the player area prior to the release of the seekers at the 18 minute mark of game time.

8.3.3.3. Once the snitch runner has been released onto the pitch, the snitch runner may not leave the player area until the snitch has been successfully caught.

8.3.3.4. The snitch runner cannot be caught until after the 18 minute mark of game time when both seekers are released onto the pitch.

8.3.4. Spectacles

Snitch runners may choose to be creative in their evasion tactics with spectacles. All spectacles are subject to the following restrictions:

A. The snitch runner must not bring any props into the player area.
B. Snitch runners must ensure that any spectacles do not hinder play outside of the seeker game.
C. Spectacles performed by the snitch runner must not delay the start of the game.
D. Spectacles must not be unfair or biased toward one team and must not detract from the role of the snitch runner as stated in 8.3.1. Role of the snitch runner.

8.3.5. The snitch runner's release

Snitch runners must report to the timekeeper at the 17 minute mark of game time and then the timekeeper will release the snitch runner into the player area prior to the 18 minute mark of game time when the seekers are released.

8.3.6. Confirming the catch

8.3.6.1. The snitch referee must blow a whistle in paired short blasts to stop play immediately when the referee believes the snitch may have been successfully caught.

8.3.6.2. If the snitch referee does not blow the whistle to stop play, the snitch runner must immediately report the catch to the head referee who must immediately stop play with paired short whistle blasts.

8.3.6.3. Any otherwise good goal made before the whistle is blown to stop play must be counted as good unless the snitch runner or another referee has clear knowledge that the successful snitch catch was made prior to the good goal.

8.3.7. Snitch requirements and code of conduct

8.3.7.1. Snitch runners must abide by the following requirements and recommendations in order to ensure the fairness of the game and the safety of the players and spectators. A snitch runner must not:

A. Intentionally injure anyone.

B. Play recklessly or dangerously.

C. Play with a bias to one team.

D. Stay near one team's side of the pitch for an extended period of time.

E. Intentionally leave the player area.

F. Intentionally touch any ball, including holding or shielding the snitch ball itself.

G. Rearrange or remove players' headbands.

H. Disobey a directive from the head referee.

I. Interact with any players other than the seekers.

J. Intentionally go to the ground, so as to be ruled as down, unless injured, unable to play, avoiding a dangerous situation, adjusting equipment, or asked to do so by a referee.

K. Intentionally pull a seeker's headband, clothing, or equipment, other than the broom.

8.3.7.2. Breach of standards by the snitch runner:

A. A referee must warn the snitch runner of violations or breaches of these standards.
    i. Major violations may warrant removal of the snitch runner without a previous warning.
B. The head referee may remove any snitch runner due to injury, breach of the standards listed in 8.3.7. Snitch requirements and code of conduct, or being overly aggressive or irresponsible.
C. If the snitch runner commits a major violation against one seeker, play should be stopped immediately and any snitch catch by the opposing team before play is stopped must be called no good.

8.3.8. Physical play and safety

The snitch runner is responsible for the safety of seekers, other players, officials, and spectators.

8.3.8.1. The rules forbidding specific types of physical contact do not apply to the snitch runner except for the following:

A. The snitch runner must not make contact with a seeker's head, neck, or groin.
    i. The snitch runner may make incidental contact with the seeker's head or neck while in the process of another move or in a playful manner (such as messing a seeker's hair).
B. The snitch runner may not make contact with a seeker's

legs at or below the knee unless contact with the seeker has already been established in another manner.

C. The snitch runner must never play recklessly or dangerously.

8.3.8.2. The snitch runner must follow the snitch code of conduct as outlined in 8.3.7. Snitch requirements and code of conduct.

8.3.8.3. The snitch runner may intentionally take a knee so as to be ruled as down if injured, unable to play, avoiding a dangerous situation, adjusting equipment, or being asked to do so by a referee.

8.3.8.4. The snitch runner should use common sense to avoid harming seekers, be aware of their surroundings, and avoid collisions with spectators.

8.3.9. Ruled as down

8.3.9.1. When the snitch runner is down, the snitch is uncatchable, regardless of whether the snitch went down intentionally or unintentionally.

A. A snitch runner is considered down when:
    i. Any part of the snitch runner's body, other than the snitch runner's hands or feet, touches the ground.
        a. The snitch sock itself touching the ground does not cause the snitch runner to be considered down, unless the sock is pinned to the ground by the snitch runner's body.
    ii. Any part of the snitch runner contacts the ground on or outside the boundary of the player area.
    iii. The snitch runner's clothing needs to be adjusted, as described in 7.5.4.C.ii

B. If the snitch runner becomes down at the exact same time the snitch is caught, the snitch runner must be ruled as down, and the catch must be ruled no good.

8.3.9.2. After a snitch runner has gone down, the seekers must:

A. Release all parts of the snitch runner's body/clothing and the snitch ball.

B. Allow the snitch runner to rise to their feet.

C. Allow the snitch runner to adjust all clothing and equipment

D. Allow an additional three-second head start as counted off by the snitch referee before they can directly pursue the snitch again.

🏴 *Penalty: Back to hoops*—A seeker who pursues the snitch runner who has been ruled as down before the three second head start has been counted off must be sent back to hoops.

9. Fouls and Misconduct

9.1. DISCIPLINARY SANCTIONS

9.1.1. Back to hoops fouls

If a player commits a foul that results in a back to hoops penalty:

A. Play should generally not be stopped.
B. A referee informs the player of the infringement and subsequent consequence.
C. If the player does not immediately comply, the referee may loudly and repetitively issue the directive to ensure that the player is aware of the instruction.
D. If at any point a referee believes that a player has had sufficient notice, but is still ignoring the directive, the referee may stop play and issue a yellow card to the offending player.

🏴 *Penalty: Yellow*—A player who ignores the referee's punishment after committing an offense that would have otherwise been a back to hoops may receive a yellow card.

9.1.2. Turnover

Turnovers without cards are generally called when a player unintentionally illegally moves a ball. Turnovers result in possession of a specific ball being given to the opposing team. If a penalty leads to a turnover without a penalty card:

A. Unless otherwise stated in the specific penalty section for the foul, the referee may choose to stop play or complete the turnover while play continues, as they deem appropriate.

B. If the referee chooses to complete the turnover without stopping play, the following procedure applies:

   i. The referee identifies the ball to be turned over and the team which is to receive the turnover.

   ii. If a player on the fouling team is holding that ball, they must immediately drop it.

      a. The player may not throw the ball, however, if the referee determines that the player is unaware of the call at the time of the throw, no further penalty shall apply for this infraction.

         1. If the ball is loose and a player on the fouling team propels it in any way, the same standards shall apply.

   iii. Whether the ball is propelled or dropped by the fouling team, the referee may pick it up and pass it to a member of the receiving team, or they may have the receiving team retrieve the ball where it lands, as they deem appropriate.

      a. If, for any reason, the situation changes and the referee determines that stopping play would be more appropriate, play may be stopped and the procedures in 9.1.2.C. shall be followed.

      b. If the ball is a bludger and all of the fouled team's beaters either already possess a bludger or are in the penalty box, then the bludger is left where it is and the fouling team may play it immediately upon the referee's signal that the bludger is clear to play.

  c. Except in the situation described in section 9.1.2.B.iii.b. above, if there are no eligible receivers because every player on the receiving team who could play the ball is either knocked out or already has a ball, the ball is instead placed next to or thrown to the center hoop of the receiving team by the referee.

iv. The receiving team must gain possession of the ball before the fouling team may contact it.

v. The fouling team may not take any action to prevent or delay the receiving team from gaining possession of the turned over ball, including beating the retrieving player.

vi. The receiving team must move immediately to gain possession of the turned over ball.

  a. Any member of the receiving team may choose to decline the ball on behalf of their team by saying "decline" or otherwise clearly signaling that they decline the ball.

   1. If the team declines the ball, the ball immediately becomes eligible to be played by members of either team.

  b. If the referee determines that no player on the receiving team is moving to gain possession of a ball to be turned over, the referee shall either verbally designate a specific eligible player without a ball to retrieve the ball or pass the ball to them as they deem appropriate.

   1. If the opposing team has set up around the ball, the designated player may choose to quickly retreat to a safer location and request that the ball be passed to them there.

      2. Once the designated player has been clearly informed of their designation by the referee, continued refusal to accept the ball shall be treated as declining the ball for their team.

vii. The fouling team may interact with the player gaining possession of the turned over ball as soon as possession is gained.

C. If the referee chooses to stop play to complete the turnover, the following procedure applies:

    i. Play is stopped.

    ii. The referee signals that there was a turnover penalty.

    iii. The referee takes the ball and gives it to the closest eligible player on the receiving team.

        a. If the ball is a bludger and all of the fouled team's beaters either already possess a bludger or are in the penalty box, then the bludger is left where it is and either team may play it immediately once play is restarted.

        b. Except in the situation described in section 9.1.2.C.iii.a. above, if there are no eligible receivers because every player on the receiving team who could play the ball is either knocked out or already has a ball, the ball is instead placed next to the center hoop of the receiving team, and it shall be treated as a continued-play-turnover at that location when play resumes.

D. A quaffle that is to be turned over cannot score for the fouling team between the time of the foul and the completion of the turnover procedure.

🏴 *Penalty: Back to hoops*—If a player on the fouling team takes any action to prevent or delay the recovery of the turned over ball, they must be sent back to hoops.

🏴 *Penalty: Yellow*—A player who the referee determines to be willfully ignoring the turnover call must receive a yellow card.

9.1.3. Blue card

Blue cards are issued for rules violations that are generally considered to be minor or technical in nature. Blue cards result in possession being turned over to the opposing team if the player who committed the foul had possession of a ball, result in a team playing down a player for one minute or until the opposing team scores, and do not stack to become yellow or red cards. If a penalty results in a blue card:

A. Play is stopped.
B. The referee signals that there was a blue card penalty by showing a blue card and communicating the nature of the foul.
C. The player who committed the foul is sent to the penalty box for one minute of game time or until the opposing team scores, whichever occurs first.
   i. The fouling team must play down a player at that position for the duration of the penalty time and the fouling player may not be substituted while in the penalty box unless they are injured or ejected.
   ii. Players may receive multiple blue cards in a single game without additional penalty.
   iii. If, at the discretion of the referee, a player is intentionally committing multiple blue card penalties, the referee may issue a yellow card for a blue card offense.

       iv. For special situations, such as receiving a blue card or yellow card while in the penalty box for a blue card, see section 9.2.2. Time of penalty.

  D. Blue card fouls result in the following turnovers:

       i. If the fouling player was in possession of the quaffle, the quaffle is turned over to the closest eligible player of the opposing team.

       ii. Any ball that the fouling player possessed or acted on from the time of the foul until play was stopped must be turned over to the opposing team's closest eligible player before play is resumed. This includes any balls that a fouled team was prevented from possessing by the foul.

       iii. If both teams have committed fouls which would turn over the same ball, possession of that ball is determined by:

         a. The foul receiving the most severe card.

         b. If multiple fouls receive the same card, among those fouls, the foul committed last.

       iv. If there is no eligible player to receive a turnover, the procedures in 9.1.2.C.iii. shall be used.

       v. If a player on the formerly defending team receives a blue card for a foul committed after the quaffle fully passed through the hoop for a good goal, but the foul was committed as part of a play to defend against the goal, the blue card shall not result in a turnover of the quaffle to the formerly offensive team.

         a. The goal does not negate the penalty time for the subsequent foul.

  E. If there was an advantage call or delayed penalty, players should be reset to the proper positions as indicated in

3.3.4. Advantage or 3.3.5. Delayed penalties.

F.   Play is resumed.

G.   The one minute of penalty time begins.

9.1.4. Yellow card

Yellow cards are issued for rules violations that are generally considered to be serious fouls. If a penalty results in a yellow card:

A.   Play is stopped.

B.   The referee signals that there was a yellow card penalty by showing a yellow card and communicating the nature of the foul.

C.   The player who committed the foul is sent to the penalty box for one minute of game time or until the opposing team scores, whichever occurs first.

  i.   The fouling team must play down a player at that position for the duration of the penalty time and the fouling player may not be substituted while in the penalty box.

  ii.   If the player is receiving a second yellow card in the same game, the player must receive a red card after being shown the yellow card. All red card procedures apply in this case (See: 9.1.5. Red card).

D.   Yellow card fouls result in the following turnovers:

  i.   If the fouling team was in possession of the quaffle, or if the quaffle is loose, the quaffle is turned over to the closest eligible player of the opposing team.

  ii.   Any bludger that the fouling player possessed or acted on from the time of the foul until play was stopped must be turned over to the opposing team's closest eligible player before play is resumed. This includes any bludgers that a fouled team was prevented from possessing by the foul.

iii. If both teams have committed fouls which would turn-over the same ball, possession of that ball is determined by:

   a. The foul receiving the most severe card.

   b. If multiple fouls receive the same card, among those fouls, the foul committed last.

iv. If there is no eligible player to receive a turnover, the procedures in 9.1.2.C.iii. shall be used.

v. If a player on the formerly defending team receives a yellow card for a foul committed after the quaffle fully passed through the hoop for a good goal, but the foul was committed as part of a play to defend against the goal, the yellow card shall not result in a turnover of the quaffle to the formerly offensive team.

   a. The goal does not negate the penalty time for the subsequent foul.

E. If there was an advantage call or delayed penalty, players should be reset to the proper positions as indicated in 3.3.4. Advantage or 3.3.5. Delayed penalties.

F. Play is resumed.

G. The one minute of penalty time begins.

9.1.5. Red card

Red cards are issued for rules violations that are generally considered to be serious enough for players to be ejected from the remainder of the game. If a penalty results in a red card:

A. Play is stopped.

B. The referee signals that there was a red card penalty by

showing a red card and communicating the nature of the foul.

C. The ejected player must leave the player area and may not return for the remainder of the game.

   i. An assistant referee or tournament official may escort the player to an appropriate location away from the field of play.

   ii. If the player refuses to leave the player area:

      a. The player's team must assist in escorting the player away from the player area.

      b. If the player persists in refusing to leave, or becomes a danger to officials, other players, or spectators, the head referee may end the game resulting in a forfeit for the fouling player's team.

   iii. The referee may choose to allow the ejected player to remain in the vicinity of the player area for the remainder of the game, as they deem appropriate, only if the red card was given for receiving two yellow cards in the game.

      a. The player must still remain outside of the player area.

      b. The player must leave the vicinity of the player area unless informed by the head referee that they may remain in the vicinity.

   iv. Ejected players must not reenter the player area.

   v. Ejected players must not attempt to communicate with anyone who is inside the player area.

D. Red card fouls result in the following turnovers:

   i. If the fouling team was in possession of the quaffle, or if the quaffle is loose, the quaffle is turned over to the closest eligible player of the opposing team.

ii. Any bludger that the fouling player possessed or acted on from the time of the foul until play was stopped must be turned over to the opposing team's closest eligible player before play is resumed. This includes any bludgers that a fouled team was prevented from possessing by the foul.

iii. If both teams have committed fouls which would turnover the same ball, possession of that ball is determined by:

    a. The foul receiving the most severe card.

    b. If multiple fouls receive the same card, among those fouls, the foul committed last.

iv. If there is no eligible player to receive a turnover, the procedures in 9.1.2.C.iii. shall be used.

v. If a player on the formerly defending team receives a red card for a foul committed after the quaffle fully passed through the hoop for a good goal, but the foul was committed as part of a play to defend against the goal, the red card shall not result in a turnover of the quaffle to the formerly offensive team.

E. The team must substitute a player in for the fouling player:

    i. The substitute for the fouling player is sent to the penalty box for two full minutes of game time.

        a. If the fouling player had time remaining in the penalty box from a previous penalty, the remaining time from that penalty is waived.

    ii. The substitute serving time for the fouling player is not released on a score.

    iii. For special situations, such as receiving a penalty while in the penalty box, see section 9.2.2. Time of penalty.

F. Play is resumed.

G. The two minutes of penalty time begin.

🏴 *Penalty: Special*—An ejected individual who communicates with anyone inside the player area must be required to leave the vicinity of the player area. Additionally, the speaking captain of the ejected individual's team must receive a yellow card. This penalty shall not apply to an individual who is simply cheering for their team.

🏴 *Penalty: Forfeit*—If an ejected individual persists in refusing to leave the player area or its vicinity after a red card, or becomes a danger to officials, other players, or spectators, the head referee may end the game resulting in a forfeit for the fouling player's team.

9.1.6. Plays after a foul

Any goal, knockout, or snitch catch performed by a player immediately after committing a foul does not count.

A. A referee's call may include sending the fouling player back to hoops, stopping play to issue a foul or card, or calling advantage.
B. For any plays during advantage or delayed penalties, see 3.3.4. and 3.3.5.2., respectively in place of this rule.

9.1.7. Fouls prior to the game

If a player is assessed a foul before Brooms Up that would result in penalty time, the foul is enforced at the beginning of the game.

A. The offending team begins the game with the offending player (or the player's replacement, in the case of a red card) in the penalty box, and the team begins with fewer than six players for Brooms Up.

B. The player's penalty time officially begins when the head referee begins the game.

9.1.8. Fouls after the game ends

If a player is assessed a foul after the game ends:

A. The penalty must be noted normally on the scorecard for the game.

B. A penalty may extend into future games if the player committed a particularly egregious red card offense, at the discretion of the tournament director after consultation with the head referee of the game and the team captains.

9.1.9. No harm no foul

In the case of a minor offense that has not given either team an advantage, a referee may decide "no harm no foul" and may choose to verbally warn players about a potential infraction rather than calling a foul.

9.1.10. Warnings

A referee may issue warnings about potential rules violations as necessary.

9.1.11. Simultaneous penalty

If a player commits two fouls simultaneously, the referee adjudicates the penalty for the more egregious foul.

9.2. THE PENALTY BOX

9.2.1. Penalty box conditions

A player or substitute is sent to a team's penalty box for any of the following offenses:

A. Receiving a blue card.
B. Receiving a yellow card.
C. Receiving a red card (player's substitute is sent to the penalty box).

9.2.2. Time of penalty

A. Blue cards and yellow cards result in one minute of game time in the penalty box for the offending player, unless the opposing team scores during that minute.
  i. When the opposing team scores by any method, the player with the least amount of penalty time remaining from a blue card or yellow card is released from the penalty box.
    a. A single goal may only count towards the release of one player.
      1. If two players on the same team have the same amount of time remaining in the penalty box for releasable penalties, the head referee shall use their discretion to designate one to be released first.
      2. If a player is serving time for two cards under 9.2.2.C.i or 9.2.2.C.ii., goals will only count towards their release if no other player on their team has less time remaining for a blue card or yellow card penalty.
B. A red card results in two full minutes of game time in

the penalty box for the offending player's replacement. A player in the penalty box for a red card may not be released due to a score.

C. Stacking penalty time:

i. In most circumstances, penalty time does not stack. If a player commits two penalties on the same play or if a second foul carries a higher penalty, the referee must adjudicate the harsher penalty.

ii. If a player serving penalty time in the penalty box for their own penalty commits a second foul:

 a. A player in the penalty box for a blue card who commits a blue or yellow card foul shall have the penalty time for the second card added to their penalty time. The player must remain in the box until the time is over or the opposing team scores two goals.

 b. A player in the penalty box for a yellow card who commits a blue card foul shall have the penalty time for the second card added to their penalty time. The player must remain in the penalty box until the time is over or the opposing team scores two goals.

 c. A player in the penalty box for a yellow card who commits a second yellow card foul shall be given a red card. The remaining time for the initial yellow is waived and the substitute must remain in the penalty box for two full minutes from the time of the second foul.

 d. For the purposes of Rule 9.2.2.C.ii., a player shall be considered "in the penalty box" from the moment they are shown the penalty card to the moment they are released from the penalty box.

iii. If a substitute serving time in the penalty box for a

different player's penalty commits a yellow, blue, or red card offense:

a. The team's speaking captain must replace the substitute with a player in active play, maintaining all aspects of 9.2.4.B., to serve the remaining time of the original penalty.

b. The substitute who committed the foul, or in the case of a red card a replacement for that substitute, must serve the full appropriate penalty time for the foul committed.

9.2.3. Proceeding to the penalty box

Play is stopped while the fouling player or appropriate substitute is sent to the penalty box.

A. If the fouling player being sent to the penalty box is in the game as a keeper, the player must switch positions with one of the chasers on their team who is in play, by switching headbands, before they go to the penalty box.

   i. This switch may be made anywhere on the pitch.

   ii. This switch must be made as quickly as possible.

B. The person going to the penalty box must proceed immediately to the penalty box without delay and remain there until the penalty expires.

   i. If a player is given a blue or yellow card, but is injured and needs to be removed from the pitch, the player may elect to be replaced in the penalty box by a substitute.

      a. If a carded player is replaced in the penalty box due to an injury, that player may not reenter play until their substitute is released from the penalty box.

   ii. A player in the penalty box may not be substituted for

any other reason.

C. Penalty time begins as soon as the head referee resumes play.

🏴 *Penalty: Yellow*—A player who does not proceed immediately to the penalty box when instructed to do so by a referee must receive a yellow card in addition to any other penalty.

🏴 *Penalty: Yellow*—If a team substitutes a player in the penalty box, then the speaking captain must receive a yellow card.

9.2.4. Penalty box considerations

A. Players in the penalty box for blue, yellow, or red card offenses are considered in play for the purposes of the gender maximum rule and positions.

B. If a player is serving time for another player's card (due to an ejection or injury) the carded player, not the player serving the time, is considered in play for the purposes of the gender maximum rule and positions for the duration of the penalty.

C. Players in the penalty box are subject to the same restrictions and penalties regarding interacting with play as substitutes (See: 6.2.6. Substitutes interfering with play).

D. Players in the penalty box may not be mounted on a broom.

9.2.5. Tracking penalty time

The timekeeper keeps track of the penalty time.

A. Penalty time begins when the referee blows the whistle to restart play.

B. As soon as a player's penalty time expires, the timekeeper must release the player from the penalty box.

i. When a player is released from the penalty box, they are considered dismounted, and they must follow the knockout procedure to reenter play.

ii. Any player serving time in the penalty box may return to play as soon as the penalty expires.

iii. Penalty time carries over into additional periods as appropriate.

9.2.6. Unusual penalty box situations

A. Substitute in the penalty box—If a team has a substitute sent to the penalty box for a blue, yellow, or red card, that team must play a player down.

  i. If a substitute is sent to the penalty box, the team's speaking captain must designate one of the players that is in play to leave the pitch.

B. Keeper sent to penalty box, no chasers in play—One keeper must be in play for each team at all times. If a keeper is sent to the penalty box, but all of that keeper's team's chasers are already in the penalty box, the keeper must trade headbands with any other player on the team who is in play, ensuring that the team still has a keeper in play.

C. Keeper sent to penalty box, no teammates in play—In the unlikely event that all other eligible players are already in the penalty box when a keeper earns penalty time, the fouling team must forfeit the game.

  i. If both teams reach this situation on the same play or incident, a double forfeit shall be declared.

🚩 *Penalty: Forfeit*—If a team has all players in play serving time in the penalty box, the fouling team must forfeit the game.

🚩 *Penalty: Forfeit*—If both teams have all players in play serving time in the penalty box, a double forfeit shall be declared.

Appendix A: Definitions

Beaters—Two players on each team who must wear black headbands and throw, kick, or in any way propel the bludgers to disrupt the flow of the game by "knocking out" other players (See: 7.4. Beater rules).

Bludgers—Three 8.5 inch diameter inflated rubber balls which may only be used by the beaters and are used to temporarily knock opponents out of play (See: 2.3.2. Bludgers).

Body blocking—A form of contact consisting of initiating force upon an opponent using body parts other than arms/hands (such as shoulders, chest, or hips). Body blocking is contact that does not use the entire force of the attacking player. In order to be a body block and not a charge, any force initiated must be after non-forceful contact has already been established with the body (See: 6.3.2.3. Body blocking).

Brooms Up—The starting words for a period of quidditch. On the "B" sound of Brooms Up, all players must mount their brooms and begin play (See: 3.2. Starting the game).

Charge—A form of physical contact which consists of turning or launching one's body directly at an opponent and forcefully bumping into them so as to halt their progress, knock them off balance, or knock them to the ground (See: 6.3.2.5. Charging).

Chasers—Three players on each team who must wear white

headbands and throw, kick, or in any way pass the quaffle through the opposing team's hoops to score 10 points and attempt to stop the other team from doing so. Chasers are quaffle players (See: 7.3. Quaffle player rules).

Dead bludger—A bludger which cannot inflict the knockout effect due to not having been propelled by an eligible beater, having hit the ground since it was last made live, traveling beyond the spectator boundary, or being in the possession of a beater (See: 5.2.2. Live bludger).

Dead quaffle—A quaffle that cannot be used to score. During the time between when a goal is confirmed as good by the head referee and when quaffle play is restarted, the quaffle is dead (See: 4.4.2. Dead quaffle).

Delay of game—An attempt to stop or significantly impede the continuation of the quaffle game (See: 3.3.6.1. Delay of game).

Free bludger—A bludger that is not in the possession of a beater on either team. If one team controls two bludgers the remaining free bludger may not be guarded and the opposing team may request immunity in an attempt to retrieve the free bludger (See: 7.4.2.6. Guarding bludgers and 7.4.3. Knockout immunity).

Gender maximum rule—The rule which allows each team to have a maximum of four players, not including the seeker, who identify as the same gender in active play on the field at the same time. (See: 7.1.3. Gender maximum rule).

Game—A singular competition between two teams for the purpose of declaring a winner. A game must follow all rules in this rulebook as well as any USQ regulations to be considered official.

Game time—The official time of any given game, measured from the first "B" sound of brooms up until the end of the final period of the game but paused for stoppages in play and between periods (See: 3.4. Regulating game time).

Good goal—Ten points are scored for a team when the quaffle in any way passes entirely through their opponent's hoops and the goal is confirmed as good (See: 4.1.1. Good goal).

Goaltending—Certain illegal actions which prevent the quaffle passing through a hoop which result in 10 points for the attacking team, as if a goal had been scored (See: 4.3. Goaltending).

Grab—A form of physical contact between players consisting of holding an opponent or any part of an opponent with a closed hand (See: 6.3.2.6. Grabbing).

Grappling—A form of physical contact between players consisting of placing a hand or hands on an opponent to jostle for position on the field (See: 6.3.2.1. Incidental contact/grappling).

Guarding a bludger—Taking any action that would prevent or significantly delay the opposing team from gaining possession of a bludger. It is illegal for a team possessing two bludgers to guard the remaining free bludger (See: 7.4.2.6. Guarding bludgers).

Helpless receiver—A receiver who is in the process of catching a ball that is in the air. The receiver does not have to leave the ground in order to be considered a helpless receiver. It is illegal to push, charge, tackle, or wrap a helpless receiver (See: 6.3.1.10. Helpless receiver).

Hoops—The upright and self supporting structure through which the quaffle must pass to score a goal. Hoops are interacted with in two ways: projecting the quaffle through the loop results in a goal and after a player is subjected to the knockout effect, that player must touch anywhere on the hoop, including the pole but not the base, before returning to play (See: 2.2. Hoops).

Intentional—An action performed with a specific purpose in mind. Many actions are illegal when performed intentionally.

Keeper—The quaffle player on each team who must wear a green headband and is a quaffle player but has special additional rules related to preventing opponents from scoring with the quaffle (See: 7.3.3. Keeper specific rules).

Kick—To strike with a foot or feet, or with any part of the leg below the knee. At the time of a kick the player striking the ball is said to have possession of that ball. A player may kick a ball they are able to play once, but it must be picked up before they may kick it again. It is illegal to kick an opponent.

Knockout immunity—A player with knockout immunity is not affected by the knockout effect. The keeper is immune in that keeper's own keeper zone until the quaffle leaves the zone. An eligible beater gains knockout immunity by raising a hand in a fist. (See: 7.4.3. Knockout immunity).

Live bludger—A bludger that has been thrown, kicked, or otherwise intentionally propelled by a beater who is in play and not knocked out. A live bludger can inflict the knockout effect upon opponents (See: 5.2.2. Live bludger).

Live quaffle—A quaffle that is eligible to score goals. The quaffle is made live by the head referee on the first sound of "B" in "Booms Up!", by the head referee with one short whistle blast after a stoppage of play, and by the keeper by gaining sole possession in their half of the pitch after their opponent scored a goal.

Natural motion—A player's continued movement in making a play, one singular natural motion that the player had already started, if that motion cannot be stopped (See: 5.3.4. Natural motion).

Opponents' keeper zone—The keeper zone containing the hoops that a team is trying to score through.

Opponents' half of the pitch—The half of the pitch containing the hoops that a team is trying to score through.

Overtime—Overtime is an extra period in a game that occurs when a snitch catch in regular time causes a game to be tied. Overtime lasts five minutes or until the snitch is caught again (See: 3.5. Overtime).

Own keeper zone—The keeper zone is the one containing the hoops that a team is trying to defend. The keeper is subject to special rules while in the keeper's own keeper zone.

Own half of the pitch—The half of the pitch containing the hoops that a team is trying to defend.

Penalty box—A 6x6 yard box bordering the midfield line, the pitch, and the player area boundary where players must remain for a certain amount of time after committing a foul. Each team has a penalty box on their own side of the midfield line. Players in the penalty area may not interact with play, but are considered in play for purposes of the gender maximum rule and positions (See: 2.1.4 The penalty box and 9.2 The penalty box).

Penalty time—The time a player must spend in the penalty box due to a foul. Penalty time is measured in game time and therefore does not run during a stoppage of play (See: 9.2.5. Tracking penalty time).

Period—A segment of a game. There may be up to three periods in any given game: regulation time, which occurs in all games; first overtime, which occurs when the teams are tied at the end of regulation time; and second overtime, which occurs when teams are tied at the end of first overtime.

Pick—An attempt to slow down an opposing player, or make them change direction by getting into a legal position in their path without initially pushing, charging, or wrapping the opponent (See: 6.3.1.3. Picks)

Pitch boundary—The pill-shaped boundary marked by parallel straight sidelines and curved backlines into which play is generally restricted (See: 2.1.1. Pitch shape).

Player area—The 72 x 48 yard (66 x 44 meter) rectangular area which includes and surrounds the pitch. All play is confined within the player area. Anything outside the player area is the spectator area (See: 2.1.8 Player and spectator areas).

Possession—Complete and sole control of a ball. A player who is intentionally kicking a ball is considered to have possession of that ball while they are the sole person in contact with the ball.

Protected Keeper—A keeper within their own keeper zone, except in the situation described in 7.3.3.1.B.

Push—A form of physical contact which consists of initiating force upon an opponent with an extended arm, be it extended during or before initiation of contact (See: 6.3.2.4. Pushing).

Quaffle—The ball used by chasers and keepers to score goals (See: 2.3.1. The quaffle).

Regulation time—The initial period of a game from the call of "Brooms Up!" until the first good snitch catch. Regulation time excludes any overtimes.

Reset—A reset, in relation to the quaffle game, is propelling the quaffle in order to retreat and regroup with it. There are limitations on resetting the quaffle into the resetting team's own half, or further away from the midline within the resetting team's own half (See: 3.3.6.2. Resetting).

Second overtime—The second overtime period is instituted if overtime ends in a tie. In second overtime, the first team to score by any method is pronounced the winner (See: 3.5.3. Second overtime).

Seeker—The player on each team who must wear a yellow headband and who attempts to remove the snitch ball from the snitch runner to score 30 points and end the game (See: 7.5. Seeker rules).

Seeker floor—The time during a period in which the snitch is ineligible to be caught. In regulation time the seeker floor is 18 minutes. In first overtime the seeker floor is 30 seconds (See: 3.4.1.2. Seeker floor and 3.5.2.G. First overtime).

Snitch—The snitch consists of a snitch runner and snitch ball. Seekers attempt to catch the snitch by removing the snitch ball from the snitch runner, thus earning 30 points and ending the game (See: 2.3.3. The snitch).

Snitch ball— The snitch ball consists of a ball and a sock and must be attached to the back of the snitch runner's shorts. Seekers attempt to remove the snitch ball to earn 30 points and end the game (See: 2.3.3. The snitch).

Snitch runner—An assistant referee who is tasked with protecting the snitch ball from being caught (See: 8.3. The snitch runner).

Speaking captain—The designated individual on the team who is the only person who may speak for the team when conversing with officials.

Spectator area—The area outside of the 72 x 48 yard (66 x 44 meter) player area where spectators may be seated. Players may never enter the spectator area, unless allowed to do so by a referee (See: 7.2.5. The spectator area).

Steal—A player's attempt to extract a ball from an opponent by either stripping or poking it loose (See: 6.3.2.2. Stealing).

Struck beater—A struck beater is a beater who has been hit by a live bludger propelled by an opponent (See: 5.2.4. Struck beater).

Substitute area—A designated zone existing outside of the pitch boundary, beginning at each keeper zone line and extending to the nearest end line, where all substitutes must remain for the duration of a game (See: 2.1.5.1. Substitute areas and 6.2.5. Substitute area).

Tackle—A form of physical contact between players consisting of wrapping a player and bringing that player to the ground (See: 6.3.2.8. Tackling).

Third bludger—See: Free bludger.

Tripping—Any attempt to knock a player off the player's feet through contact below the knees. Tripping is always illegal physical contact (See: 6.3.1.2.K.).

Unscorable quaffle—If a player is touching a quaffle when struck by a live bludger and releases it or propels the it according to natural motion, the quaffle becomes an unscorable quaffle. An unscorable quaffle cannot result in a goal, even if the quaffle goes entirely through a hoop (See: 5.3.4.2. Unscorable quaffle).

Wrap—A wrap consists of encircling an opponent's torso or any part of an opponent with an arm or arms (See: 6.3.2.7. Wrapping).

Appendix B: List of Fouls by Type

B-1. INDIVIDUAL FOULS

B-1.1. Special

> 2.5.2. Players deemed to be wearing illegal headbands must immediately leave the pitch and correct the headband or be replaced by a player with a proper headband.

B-1.2. Warning offenses

A referee may issue a warning to players for certain offenses that the referee considers to be "no harm, no foul" (See: 9.1.9. No Harm, No Foul) and may warn players at any time in an attempt to prevent illegal actions from occurring (See: 9.1.10. Warnings). The following are specific warning offenses:

> 3.3.6.1. Delay of game (can also be a blue card).
> 6.1.2.2. Using undirected explicit, vulgar, or abusive language (first offense).

B-1.3. Repeat offenses

The following are offenses for which the offending player must repeat the action properly before continuing with play:

> 5.3.1. Failing to dismount, or remounting before touch-

ing the hoops, during the knockout procedure.

6.2.2.1. Violating the substitution procedure.

6.2.3. Illegally changing positions with a teammate.

B-1.4. Back to hoops offenses

The referee must send any player who commits any of the following offenses back to that player's hoops with the player completing all of the knockout procedure as described in section 5.3. The following are back to hoops offenses:

2.5.6. Failing to replace a lost headband at a stoppage of play.

5.1.2. Dismounting while in play.

5.2.8.1. Failing to give up immunity when both beaters have claimed it (only one beater is penalized).

5.2.8.1. Unintentionally illegally claiming immunity without affecting gameplay.

5.2.8.2. Manipulating immunity.

6.3.1.2. Unintentionally making illegal contact and adjusting immediately, when gameplay was not affected.

6.3.1.3. Setting an unintentionally illegal pick and adjusting immediately, when gameplay was not affected.

6.3.1.6. Unintentionally making initial contact from behind and adjusting immediately, when gameplay was not affected.

6.3.1.9. Unintentionally illegally sliding or diving and adjusting immediately, when gameplay was not affected.

6.3.2. Unintentionally committing illegal grappling, stealing, body blocking, pushing, charging, grabbing, wrapping, or tackling, and adjusting immediately, when gameplay was not affected.

6.3.3. Being "at fault" for an illegal interpositional inter-action, when judged to be unaware of the other player and gameplay is unaffected.

7.2.2.2. Attempting and failing to avoid contact with a propelled quaffle which the player must avoid, when gameplay is not affected.

7.2.3.2. Illegally and intentionally leaving the pitch or remaining off the pitch.

7.2.3.2. Illegally altering one's path to angle further away from the pitch while off pitch.

7.2.4.2. Illegally and intentionally carrying a ball off or away from the pitch.

7.2.4.2. Illegally propelling a ball off the pitch, laterally from the pitch, or further away from the pitch while off pitch (also a turnover).

7.2.5.1. Illegally contacting the ground on or outside of the player area boundary without being physically forced.

7.4.2.6. Guarding the third bludger.

8.3.9.2. Pursuing the snitch runner who has been ruled as down before the three second head start has been counted off.

9.1.2. Taking any action to prevent or delay an opponent's recovery of a turned over ball.

B-1.5. Turnover

The following offenses result in a turnover of either a quaffle or a bludger:

3.3.6.2. Illegally resetting the quaffle (must be turned

over at the point from which the quaffle was reset).

5.3.2. Releasing a pass, shot, or beat attempt after having been knocked out, except in cases of natural motion.

5.3.4.1. Unintentionally illegally propelling a ball after being knocked out

7.2.4.2. Illegally propelling a ball off the pitch, laterally from the pitch, or further away from the pitch while off pitch (also a back to hoops).

7.3.2.3. Unintentionally acting on a bludger, as a quaffle player, in a manner that significantly affects the position of the bludger.

7.4.2.5. Unintentionally acting on the quaffle, as a beater, in a manner that significantly affects the position of the bludger.

7.4.4.2. Unintentionally acting on a quaffle with a held bludger.

7.5.3.1. Unintentionally acting on a bludger or quaffle in a manner that significantly affects the position of the ball (as a seeker).

B-1.6. Blue card

The following are blue card offenses:

2.5.2. Entering play without required equipment.

2.5.3. Using illegal equipment after the game has started.

3.2.1. Changing positions on the starting line after the referee has called "Brooms Down!"

3.2.1. Touching the ground across the starting line, or failing to reset the broom flat on the ground, before the call of "Broom's Up."

3.3.6.1. Delay of Game (can also be a warning).

3.4.1.2. Leaving the penalty box as a seeker before the seeker floor ends for that period. (Penalty time begins at the end of the seeker floor).

3.4.1.2. Entering the game as the team's initial seeker in the period without checking in with the timekeeper and being released from the penalty box.

4.2.2. Repeatedly unintentionally dislodging a hoop.

4.4.2. Intentionally illegally interacting with a dead quaffle.

5.1.2. Continuing to play after being dismounted and affecting play.

5.2.3. Intentionally holding a bludger against an opponent to make them believe they are knocked out.

5.2.4.1. Intentionally changing, or making contact in an attempt to change, the direction of a bludger after becoming a struck beater, except during an attempt to catch the bludger.

5.2.6. Illegally swatting a bludger as a chaser, keeper, or seeker.

5.2.8.1. Illegally claiming immunity, and affecting gameplay.

5.2.8.1. Knowingly illegally claiming immunity.

5.2.8.1. Raising a closed fist and taking any action other than attempting to recover the free bludger.

5.3.1. Interacting with play without completing the knockout procedure.

5.3.3. Unintentionally continuing play after being hit with a live bludger and affecting play, other than cases of throwing a ball or initiating physical contact.

6.1.2.2. Using undirected explicit, vulgar, or abusive language after being warned.

6.2.2.1. Entering the pitch as a result of an illegal substitution and either ignoring a referee's command to repeat the procedure or interacting with a ball or opponent.

6.2.3. Participating in an illegal position change which is not corrected before one of the players interacts with play. Both player receive blue cards.

6.2.5. Intentionally and illegally leaving the substitute area and affecting play.

6.2.5. Intentionally and illegally leaving the substitute area to circumvent other rules.

6.2.6. Failing to make every reasonable effort to move out of the way of play as a substitute.

7.2.2.1. Using a ball to mimic the actions of a ball of a different position.

7.2.2.1. Using a possessed or propelled ball with the intent of interacting with the snitch runner.

7.2.2.2. Illegally interacting with a quaffle by failing to attempt to avoid it, or in a way that affects gameplay.

7.2.2.2. Illegally swatting a bludger.

7.2.3.1. Illegally leaving the player area to make a play.

7.3.2.3. Using the quaffle illegally, as a quaffle player.

7.4.2.2. Performing an illegal second kick on a bludger (as a beater).

7.4.2.4. Illegally interacting with a bludger (as a beater).

7.4.2.5. Illegally possessing two bludgers (as a beater).

8.1.1.1. Disrespecting an official (can also be yellow).

8.1.2. Using verbal or visual referee commands.

B-1.7. Yellow card

The following are yellow card offenses:

2.5.2. Ignoring the directive "illegal headband."

2.5.4. Reentering the pitch without correcting an equipment infringement after being required to leave the pitch to correct that infringement.

3.3.1. Continuing to move intentionally during a stoppage, or refusing to follow a referee's instruction to return to their position at the time of a stoppage.

3.3.1. Illegally picking up or taking hold of a ball with the intent to deceive an official into believing it was held or possessed prior to the stoppage.

4.2.2. Recklessly dislodging a hoop.

5.1.2. Continuing or initiating physical contact while dismounted.

5.3.1. Intentionally or repeatedly failing to complete any part of the knockout procedure.

5.3.2. Initiating physical contact, other than incidental contact or in the final singular natural motion, while knocked out or as a struck beater.

5.3.3. Willfully ignoring being knocked out.

5.3.4.1. Intentionally beginning an illegal action with knowledge of being knocked out.

6.1.1.2. Refusing to comply with a referee's directive.

6.1.2.1. Taunting opponents.

6.1.2.1. Engaging in rude or antagonistic behavior with players, spectators, officials, or event staff.

6.1.2.2. Using explicit language or gestures directed

toward any person.

6.1.2.5. Pretending to be fouled.

6.2.4. Feigning injury

6.3.1.Making illegal physical contact either intentionally, without immediately adjusting, or in a way that affects gameplay.

6.3.1.3. Setting an illegal pick either intentionally, without immediately adjusting, or in a way that affects gameplay.

6.3.1.4. Playing recklessly.

6.3.1.4. Kicking an opponent while attempting to kick a ball.

6.3.1.6. Making initial contact from behind either intentionally, without immediately adjusting, or in a way that affects gameplay.

6.3.1.8. Failing to readjust or discontinue contact when forced into an illegal position by the actions of an opponent.

6.3.1.9. Illegally sliding or diving either intentionally, without immediately adjusting, or in a way that affects gameplay.

6.3.2. Illegally grappling, stealing, body blocking, pushing, charging, grabbing, wrapping, or tackling, either intentionally, without immediately adjusting, or in a way that affects gameplay.

6.3.3. Being "at fault" for an illegal interpositional interaction that is either intentional or affects gameplay.

7.1.2.1. Targeting the the opposing speaking captain, who is on the pitch while not in play, in an attempt to draw a card on the speaking captain for interfering with play.

7.2.2.2. Intentionally illegally interacting with a ball of another position.

7.2.2.2. Illegally interacting with a propelled quaffle in a way that blocks a score.

7.2.2.3-4. Failing to make a reasonable effort to avoid interacting with a ball in play, as a substitute or knocked out player.

7.2.4.2. Propelling a ball with the intent of sending it out of the player area.

7.2.4.2. Intentionally carrying a ball out of the player area.

7.2.5.1. Physically forcing another player into the spectator area.

7.2.5.1. Initiating contact with a player while outside of the player area.

7.2.5.2. Disregarding a referee's instruction regarding entering the spectator area.

7.2.6.2. Recklessly endangering a spectator.

7.2.7. Playing recklessly.

7.3.2.3. Intentionally illegally interacting with a bludger, as a quaffle player.

7.4.2.5. Possessing or intentionally interacting with the quaffle illegally (as a beater).

7.4.4.2. Intentionally using a held bludger to affect the trajectory of the quaffle.

7.5.3.1. Intentionally interacting with a bludger or quaffle (as a seeker).

7.5.4. Pushing, grabbing, holding, charging, wrapping,

or tackling the snitch runner (as a seeker).

8.1.1.1. Disrespecting an official (can also be blue).

8.1.1.1. Disregarding the directives of any official.

9.1.1. Ignoring the referee's punishment after committing an offense that would have otherwise been a back to hoops.

9.1.2. Willfully ignoring a turnover call.

9.2.3. Failing to proceed to the penalty box when instructed to do so.

B-1.8. Red card

The following are red card offenses:

2.4.2. Knowingly initiating a new play of any kind with a broken broom.

2.5.1. Using illegal equipment that was specifically barred in section 2.5.

2.5.3. Using illegal equipment that was specifically barred by the referee or tournament director before the game began, during ground rules, or at any previous point during the game.

2.5.5. Intentionally altering any game equipment in order to gain an advantage.

4.2.2. Intentionally dislodging a hoop.

4.2.2. Affecting the position of a hoop with the intent of affecting whether the quaffle will pass through it.

4.3. Intentionally goaltending while in play as a beater or seeker.

6.1.2.1. Directing explicit or threatening taunts toward opponents.

6.1.2.1. Engaging in explicitly rude or hostile behavior

toward players, spectators, officials, or event staff.

6.1.2.2. Using extreme or abusive language or obscene gestures directed toward any person.

6.1.2.3. Engaging in physical altercations with or threatening any players, spectators, officials, or event staff.

6.1.2.4. Committing serious foul play.

6.2.6. Intentionally interacting with play as a substitute.

6.2.7. Intentionally breaking the substitution rules in order to affect gameplay.

6.3.1.2. Making illegal contact in a way that the referee determines to be violent or egregious conduct.

6.3.1.4. Kicking an opponent in a manner that the referee determines to be violent or egregious conduct.

6.3.1.5. Making egregiously illegal physical contact.

6.3.1.6. Making initial contact from behind in a way that the referee determines to be violent or egregious conduct.

6.3.1.9. Illegally sliding or diving in a way that the referee determines to be violent or egregious conduct.

6.3.1.10. Charging or tackling a helpless receiver.

6.3.2. Illegally grappling, stealing, body blocking, pushing, charging, grabbing, wrapping, or tackling, in a way that the referee determines to be violent or egregious conduct.

6.3.3. Committing an illegal interpositional interaction in a way that the referee determines to be violent or egregious conduct.

7.2.2.2-4. Illegally and intentionally blocking the quaffle from scoring.

7.2.5.1. Initiating contact with another player while

outside the player area in a manner that the referee determines to be violent or egregious conduct.

7.2.7. Participating in particularly egregious reckless play.

B-2. SPEAKING CAPTAIN PENALTIES

Except where explicitly listed, speaking captains are subject to the same penalties as players. These are the penalties that are specific to speaking captains:

B-2.1. Speaking captain blue cards

2.5.2. Having a player in play with an illegal jersey number.

2.5.2. Having multiple players on the team in the player area wearing the same number.

7.1.2.1. Unintentionally interfering with play while on the pitch and not in play.

B-2.2. Speaking captain yellow cards

7.1.1. Intentionally failing to send a seeker into the game.

7.1.2.1. Continuing to converse with a referee after the referee has asked them to stop, or otherwise ignoring a referee's instruction.

7.1.3. Having an illegal player or set of players in play, in terms of eligibility, gender, number of players, or position.

9.1.5. Having an ejected player who is communicating

Appendix C: Referee Signals

Goal
One long whistle blast.
Two arms raised straight up.

No goal or bad snitch catch
Two arms out at the sides.

Own zone keeper possession
Yell "keeper." Arms crossed at shoulder level, fists clenched.

Good snitch catch
Three long whistle blasts.
Wave both arms above head once per whistle.

Knocked out
Yell "beat," player's jersey color, and number. Point at player's own hoops with two fingers.

Stop play
Paired whistle blasts.
One arm raised straight up.

Resume/restart play
One short whistle blast.
One-armed chopping motion.

Advantage to fouled team
One arm raised straight up. Drop marker at location of the quaffle, if quaffle advantage. Stop play after advantage.

Warning
Hold one arm, palm outward, to offending player.

Back to hoops
Yell "back."

Blue, yellow or red card
Extend arm, point at player with two fingers. State foul. Show card to player, then scorekeeper. Hold up one finger (yellow card or technical foul) or two fingers (red card) for penalty time.

General illegal contact
Fist chopping arm above head.

Illegal procedure
Roll arms in front of body.

Illegal interaction
Make a T with arms, one fist directly under other forearm.

Unsportsmanlike conduct
Hands at hips.

Illegal physical action
Mime action.

Delay of game
Tap wrist.

Substitute/bench foul
Point to offending bench with both arms.

Illegal contact to body part
Chop fouled body part with arm.

Illegal contact using body part
Point to own body part.

Becoming a Certified Referee or Snitch

USQ offers training and certification for referees and snitches. A certified head referee and lead assistant referee is paid per game and is required in order for any game to count as USQ official. Certified snitches are not required for official games, but certified snitches are paid for official games they officiate.

To learn more, visit usquidditch.org/get-involved/officials/

Appendix D: Starting a Team

So you want to start a quidditch team? Great! There have never been more resources available or a larger player community to help you out. While the process of successfully starting a team is outside the scope of this rulebook, here are a few pointers. Visit usquidditch.org/resources/ for more comprehensive information.

Get your friends on board—While your friends might not ultimately become your team's US Quidditch Cup tournament roster, they're a great place to start. Convince them to come to your first practices and help you find and make equipment.

Find equipment—There are a few options for a new team regarding purchasing or procuring equipment. Your first set of equipment doesn't need to look good; it just needs to get the job done. All you need is 14 lengths of PVC pipe or lobby brooms (you can even get away with "BYOB" for awhile), a volleyball, three dodgeballs, a tennis ball, a sock (for the snitch runner), and three hula hoops attached to just about anything for starting hoops. It's useful to have two sets of pinnies to distinguish between scrimmage teams and headbands to distinguish between positions, but they aren't necessary right away. When you're ready to upgrade, there are resources on the USQ website to help.

Promote your team—Create a team email address and Facebook page. Invite everyone you know and update it often. If you're looking to start a college team, post flyers all over campus and hold practices in high-traffic areas. Find out how to become a student organization or sport club on campus; this will bring much more visibility and often funding. Once you are a school organization, don't miss club fairs and especially new student orientation. Incoming freshmen are looking for extracurricular activities and many are looking to play intramural or club sports in college.

Reach out to other teams—Are there other quidditch teams near you? If so, email or Facebook them! Ask if you can attend their practices or if they'll play a best out of three series with you. If you don't know if there are teams near you, contact your USQ regional coordinator through the USQ website.

Don't do it alone—Once you've got people regularly showing up to practices, identify anyone with leadership potential. Put together an executive board to help run your team. Many e-boards consist of a president, vice president, secretary, treasurer, and team captain, but these roles can be adapted and more can be added as your team grows.

Fundraise—We call this "using other people's money to buy brooms." Everyone loves clever t-shirts, so quidditch shirt fundraisers are usually a big success. Bake sales, communal garage sales, and car washes are also tried and true options. Many quidditch teams host very successful "Yule Balls" open to the whole community, as well as crowd funding campaigns through such platforms as IndieGoGo and Generosity.

Use those funds to start attending and hosting tournaments—Attending tournaments is one of the best ways to get your team to bond. There's nothing quite like the atmosphere of a quidditch tournament. You'll meet tons of other players who will become instant friends and mentors for your team, and you'll get the competition experience that will motivate your team to keep practicing and training.

Join USQ—USQ offers two types of membership: team memberships for university, secondary school, or community team registration, and individual membership for players and non-playing coaches. Players who plan on competing on an official tournament team will need an individual membership as well. USQ also offers a special fan membership for the ultimate quidditch fan experience.

Team benefits include:
- Ranking on the USQ website and a team page.
- Discounted or free registration to sanctioned events.
- Ability to apply for USQ grants.
- Eligibility to compete at regionals and national championships.
- Priority support from USQ staff.

Individual membership benefits include:
- Eligibility to play on an official team and compete in official matches, as well as participate in USQ-sanctioned events.
- Insurance coverage while participating in any official matches, as well as USQ-sanctioned events in the U.S.
- Free registration for regional championships and ability to compete to qualify for the national championship.
- Player ID card for entry to USQ events.
- Official USQ member patch.
- Participation in league-wide polls.

Visit www.usquidditch.org/get-involved/membership/ for more information or to register.

Appendix E: Changelog

NOTABLE CHANGES

Changes to field dimensions, marking, and equipment

2.1.4.2. (Deleted) Scorekeepers are no longer able to modify location, shape, or size of penalty area.

2.1.6. The ball positions closest to the midpoint (internal ball marks) have been moved out an additional 1.5 yards, creating even spacing between all four balls on brooms up.

2.1.8.1. The player area length is reduced to 72 yards.

2.1.9. Starting lines have been moved from recommended line markings to required to be marked on all pitches.

2.2.1.1. Metal and concrete are banned as base materials for hoops, even when padded, save for metal fasteners.

2.4.1. Brooms now must be made of wood or plastic.

Changes to Referee Procedures

2.1.7.2.B. (Deleted). Referees are no longer able to set alternate starting lines.

2.5.7. Procedure added for jersey numbers damaged in play.

3.3.1.F.ii.b. When a bludger is to be turned over to the opposing team, but that team's beaters all have bludgers, the bludger shall remain where it is. (This is different from what happens if one of the opposing team's beaters is knocked out and returning to their hoops).

3.3.2.H.ii.b. The standard for stopping play for a non-fixable broken hoop has been changed from whether it would disadvantage the team with the quaffle to whether the hoops are being attacked by a team which has crossed midfield.

3.3.4. The head referee may send the fouling player back to hoops during an advantage for a blue, yellow, or red card foul if the situation warrants such action.

3.3.4.B. Seeker-only fouls do not activate advantage, even if called by the head referee. Their own specific procedure applies.

3.3.4.2.B.i. & 3.3.5.1.D. When multiple fouls would turn over the same ball, possession of the ball is now determined by level of card for the penalty, before the order in which they occurred.

3.3.5.1.B. Officials who are calling delayed penalties no longer have to send the fouling player back to hoops, but may do so if the situation warrants.

3.3.5.1.C.ii.a. The head referee must raise their hand upon recognizing a delayed penalty if they allow play to continue.

3.5.2.I. Delayed penalties stop the overtime clock as soon as the HR raises their hand in response.

3.6.2.2.A. If a player who was in play at the time a game was suspended has to leave before the game can be resumed, a substitute can take the field in their place upon the resumption of play.

3.6.2.2.B. Any balls which were not possessed at the time a game was suspended are placed on the ball marks for the resumption of play.

4.5.1. Impediment of the snitch runner by a game official is now a reason to dismiss a catch. The rule also clarifies that the impediment must be physical (not mental).

5.2.7. The friendly fire section has been subsumed under a new "safe calls" section. A safe call procedure has been created, expanding allowable remounts to all safe calls.

6.2.1.D.vi & 6.2.4.C.iv. If an injured player is the last player at their position, and there are no substitutes available, a player of another position switches to the injured player's position and location.

7.2.5.2.C.iii. (Deleted) The special provisions and procedures for quaffle out of bounds turnovers inside the offensive keeper zone have been eliminated.

9.1.2. The turn over procedure has been overhauled, including specific procedures for turnovers while play continues, and is applicable to more turnover penalties. Penalties for interference with a turnover have also been added.

9.1.3-5.D.v. If a player receives a penalty which would normally turn over the quaffle, but the foul occurred after a goal as part of the play to defend the goal, the quaffle shall not be turned over. However, the goal cannot negate that penalty time.

9.1.5.C.iii-v. Players who receive a red card for receiving two yellow cards in a game, may be allowed to stay in the vicinity of the player area at the discretion of the head referee. However, they must still remain outside the player area. However, they must not communicate with anyone inside the player area.

Changes to personal equipment

2.5.2.B.iii. Legal headgear in the shape of a band in a positional color shall be simply considered to be a headband. This may be worn only for the position applicable to the color of the headgear, and may not be covered up by another headband.

2.5.2.F. Minimum requirements for legal mouthguards have been added.

2.5.3.F. Hand and and glove grip enhancers which might transfer to and affect the ball are specifically banned.

Changes to gameplay and player procedures

3.3.1.J.ii. Players now must stand upon the call to remount. They may not remain on the ground.

3.3.1.J.ii.a. If two players both have a grip on the ball when the whistle blows, they must both stand with the ball. Each may take new hold of the ball upon standing, but the players do not need need to do so in the same way or in the same proportion.

3.4.1.2. The requirement for the initial seeker to report to the timekeeper prior to 17 minutes has been replaced by a requirement for the initial seeker to report to the timekeeper before entering the game through the penalty area. A penalty for entering illegally has been added, and overtime policies have been changed to match.

4.2.1. Falling hoops are considered fully dislodged (and no longer eligible to be scored on) when the hoop loop touches the ground, or the hoop comes to rest in a non-upright position.

4.2.2.C. The exception to the rules on recklessly or repeatedly dislodging a hoop during attempts to score or block a score has been modified. The exception is now limited to offensive players on contested scores and defensive players knocked into the hoop as a result of interacting with the player attempting to score.

4.4.2.B. The scoring team is now banned from interacting with the quaffle after the score is confirmed, even to pass it to the formerly defending team, unless the formerly defending team requests that they pass the quaffle to them. The scoring team may still decline request.

4.5.3. Teams have been given a limited ability to decline their own snitch catch. This is limited to when the head referee changes their stated pre-catch call on a goal after the catch occurs, and the change affects whether the period ends in a tie.

6.3.1.2.F. "Making forcible contact using the crown of the head" has been specifically added to illegal physical contact.

6.3.1.3. Picks have been redefined and the standards and penalties for picks have been specified.

6.3.1.4. Specific standards have been set for kicking a contested ball.

6.3.1.6.C-D. The standard for activating the spin rule has been changed from whether the spinning player was attempting to draw a foul to whether the spin causes the opposing player to make contact from behind, based on whether the player has time to avoid contact after the spin.

6.3.2.5.B.ii. The exception to the single point charge rule for shoulder to shoulder contact has been further restricted to "point of shoulder to point of shoulder contact" eliminating charges where the point of the shoulder hits the opponent elsewhere in the shoulder region.

6.3.3. Standards for interposition right of way have been set.

7.1.1.A.ii.b. The requirement for the minimum number of eligible players during a game has been increased from one keeper in play to one player at each active position (counting those in the penalty area).

7.1.3. Once the seeker floor for a period has ended, the seeker counts in the gender maximum rule, and up to five players of a single gender may be in play. The gender maximum rule in 1.5. has also been changed to reflect this.

7.2.2.2. The rules governing interaction with balls of other positions have been significantly expanded.

7.2.3.2.F. Players may leave the pitch to circumvent opponents, but their path, once they are off the pitch, is restricted.

7.2.3.2.D.ii. (Deleted) The requirement to not force a player further off the pitch after forcing them off the pitch has been eliminated.

7.2.4.2. A player may carry a ball with them when leaving the pitch under 7.2.3.2.F.

7.2.5.1. Players may no longer physically force other players into the spectator area.

Changes to snitch runner rules and procedures

3.4.1.3. The existence, order, and timing of the snitch handicaps are now specifically set in the rulebook. Handicaps must be used as listed. No additional handicaps may be set by tournament staff or referees. They are as follows:

> Upon release of the seekers, snitch remains between the keeper zone lines.
>
> After 23 minutes, snitch remains within 1.5 yards of the midline.
>
> After 28 minutes, snitch is limited to using only one arm.
>
> After 33 minutes, snitch remains within 1.5 yards of the intersection of the pitch sideline and the midline opposite the scorekeeper.

8.3.3.1. The snitch runner is instructed to remain in the vicinity of the pitch during the seeker floor.

8.3.4. Snitches have been banned from bringing props into the player area.

8.3.9.1.A.ii. A snitch runner touching the ground outside or on the boundary of the player area is considered down.

Penalty adjustments

2.5.2. Specific penalties added for illegal or duplicate jersey numbers.

2.5.2. Missing required equipment is now specifically a blue card.

3.2.1. False starting has been split into two parts. If the player crosses the line and touches the ground, it's an automatic blue card with no chance to reset. Picking up one's broom early without touching the ground on the other side of the line is only a blue card if they do not reset before the brooms up call.

3.3.6.1. The delay of game penalties have been modified to allow multiple warnings, as well as allowing for the blue card to be given without warning, both as the referee deems appropriate.

3.6.1.1.C. Falling below four eligible players during a game results in the game being forfeited. (up from the former minimum of one).

4.2.2.E. Moving, tilting, or spinning a hoop with the intent of affecting whether the quaffle will pass through it is now a red card offense.

5.2.4.1. Attempting and failing to swat a bludger as a struck beater is penalized the same as a successful swat.

5.2.5. The penalty for using the quaffle to interact with a dead bludger has been changed to using the quaffle to interact with a bludger the player was reasonably aware to be dead or made live by a teammate.

5.2.7.C. No penalty shall be given for failing to dismount if the final call is "safe," but believing that the call would be "safe" cannot negate or mitigate any applicable card if the call is "beat."

5.2.8.1. Back to hoops may be applied when player unintentionally illegally claims immunity without affecting gameplay. A blue card is required if gameplay is affected or the player knowingly illegally claimed immunity.

5.3.2. & 5.3.4.1. The specific turnover procedure for these penalties have been removed; they now follow the new turnover procedure section.

6.2.5. Penalty. Eliminated automatic blue card for leaving the substitute or bench area. Now listed as "may" when gameplay is affected. A blue card must be given if the player left with the intent of circumventing other rules.

7.1.2.1. Penalty. Unintentional speaking captain interference has been reduced to blue. Intentional speaking captain interference has been increased to a red. A yellow card penalty has been added for attempting to draw a speaking captain interference penalty by targeting the speaking captain.

7.2.2.1. The penalty for using a ball to mimic the actions of another ball has been reduced to a blue card. Propelling a ball with the intent of interacting with the snitch runner is also now specifically a blue card.

7.2.5.1. A back to hoops penalty has been added for illegally stepping out of the player area.

Additions made for notable clarifications

These notes do not represent changes to the meaning of the rules, but rather changes intended to clarify the meaning of the rules which already existed.

2.5. The red card penalty for explicitly barred equipment applies regardless of whether the player was warned by the head referee about the specific equipment before the player entered the game.

3.3.4.3. A legal snitch catch by the non-fouling team during advantage or a delayed penalty nullifies penalty time in the same manner as a goal.

3.3.4.4.B.ii.a. All players who commit fouls during advantage must be penalized.

3.3.5.1. The determining factor for whether there is a delayed penalty is if the head referee is the official calling the foul, not time, position, or possession.

3.3.6.1.B.iii. Carrying the quaffle to the sideline when subbing is explicitly listed as a form of delay of game.

3.3.6.1.C. A keeper subbing out after a goal before restarting the quaffle is explicitly listed as delay of game.

3.3.6.2. A referee may not opt to turn over the quaffle at its new location on a reset, however they may call no harm no foul on a reset and allow play to continue if doing so is advantageous to the opposing team.

3.5.2.I. The clocks in overtime are stopped during an advantage or delayed penalty when the head referee raises their arm or releases their advantage marker, whichever comes first.

4.3. A non-quaffle player who intentionally goaltends must receive a red card.

4.4.2.A. Substitutes may pass a dead quaffle to their keeper after a score, but must remain in the substitute area or team bench while doing so.

4.4.2.D. If a penalty turns over a dead quaffle to the formerly offensive team, the quaffle becomes live upon the restart.

6.2.2.D. A player must step onto the pitch to complete a substitution, even if play is occurring off pitch.

6.3.1.2.O. "Carrying any player" has been changed to "Lifting or continuing to hold another player off the ground."

6.3.2.6.A.iii. It is legal to intentionally cause an opponent to dismount by otherwise legally grabbing that opponent. Grabbing the broom directly is prohibited.

7.3.2.3.B.i & 7.4.2.4.B.i. Blocking a live bludger with a held ball does not negate the knockout effect from subsequent contact by that bludger while it remains live.

8.2.3.4. The snitch referee must not provide any advice or warnings to the snitch runner during the game to help them avoid being caught, including but not limited to the locations, substitutions, and tactics of the seekers.

9.2.2.C.ii.d. A player is considered "in the penalty box" from the moment they are shown their penalty card, for the purposes of determining whether a second foul results in stacking penalty time.

with anyone inside the player area.

9.2.3. Illegally substituting a player in the penalty box.

B-2.3. Speaking captain red cards

6.1.2.4. The team commits serious foul play which cannot be attributed to a specific player.

7.1.2.1. Intentionally interfering with play while on the pitch and not in play.

B-3. Forfeit offenses

Certain team or individual offenses can result in the referee calling a forfeit against the offending team. The following are reasons to call a forfeit:

3.6.1.1. Having fewer than 4 remaining eligible players (including those in the penalty box).

9.1.5. Having an ejected player who persists in refusing to leave the pitch, or becomes a danger to officials, players, or spectators.

9.2.6. Having all players in play be serving time in the penalty box.

48321766R00132

Made in the USA
San Bernardino, CA
22 April 2017